Wooden Spoon Society

RUGBY WORLD '00

EDITED BY

Nigel Starmer-Smith
and Ian Robertson

Queen Anne Press

A QUEEN ANNE PRESS BOOK

© Lennard Associates Limited 1999

First published in 1999 by
Queen Anne Press, a division of
Lennard Associates Limited
Mackerye End
Harpenden, Herts AL5 5DR

A catalogue entry is available from the British Library

ISBN 1 85291 611 7 (paperback)
ISBN 1 85291 610 9 (hardback)

Production Editor: Chris Marshall
Cover Design/Design Consultant: Paul Cooper
Reproduction: Colour Image
Printed and bound in Slovenia

The publishers would like to thank Colorsport and SpedeGrafix for
providing most of the photographs for this book.

The publishers would also like to thank Allsport, David Gibson
(Fotsport), Tony Hickey, Terry Sellick and Chris Thau for additional
material.

CONTENTS

We're proud to support
the Wooden Spoon Society.

Lloyds TSB
Official Sponsor
iRB
RUGBY
WORLD CUP
1999

 Lloyds TSB
Your life. Your bank.

FOREWORD

BY HRH THE PRINCESS ROYAL

BUCKINGHAM PALACE

It gives me great pleasure to write the foreword to this book which reflects yet again the involvement of the Wooden Spoon Society with the game of Rugby.

As Patron of the Society, I am delighted to give recognition to the considerable number and variety of projects they successfully undertake each year for the benefit of many children and young people in the United Kingdom who are otherwise disadvantaged.

I was pleased to see the opening this year of the first of two Wooden Spoon Society Teenage Cancer Trust Units, one in Manchester and the other in Birmingham. I was equally delighted at the foundation of the Wooden Spoon Society Young Carers Trust administered by my own charity The Princess Royal Trust for Carers.

In the game of rugby the Wooden Spoon sponsored New Image Rugby for Players of All Abilities grows apace bringing the thrill and spills of the game to youngsters who would normally not aspire to play the game at all.

Rugby Football is a game of great commitment requiring reserves of energy, enthusiasm and skill that are translated into a physically demanding and invariably exciting spectacle.

The Members of the Wooden Spoon Society bring the same attributes to their fund-raising activities for the benefit of others.

Please enjoy this book but also support the Charity which created it and extend your enjoyment beyond these pages into the work of the Wooden Spoon Society.

Anne

Wooden Spoon Society
- the Charity of British Rugby

Royal Patron: HRH The Princess Royal
Patrons: Rugby Football Union • Scottish Rugby Union
Welsh Rugby Union • Irish Rugby Football Union

One of the problems of being young is that quite often you are seen and not heard. This is the ideal situation for children but perhaps not for charities. While being seen is an invaluable way to be recognised, being heard is the means of communication that can lead to that glowing light at the end of the tunnel.

Because of our youth – born in 1983 but effective, as a national charity, only in this past decade – many people may have seen Wooden Spoon Society but apparently few have heard of us. This past rugby season has therefore been a momentous one for Wooden Spoon Society because so many more people now have heard of us – as well as having seen our 'horrendous' tie.

In September we had that magnificent Tribute to the Great Cliff Morgan, when, despite his protestations of 'nobody will want to listen to me', we packed 1,300 people into the London Hilton Hotel. We turned away a further 350 who really did want to listen to what he had to say. And what a tribute we gave him. The speakers ranged from the Chairman Tony (the soup kitchen man from Philadelphia) O'Reilly, through media colleagues Sir Paul Fox (BBC & ITV), David Coleman and Harry Carpenter and fellow TV colleagues from 'A Question of Sport', Henry Cooper, Mary Peters and Gareth Edwards, to a plethora of rugby giants headed by WRU President Sir Tasker Watkins and, all the way from his home in Africa, the inimitable Dr Jack Kyle, supported by Dr Jack Matthews, Bleddyn Williams, Barry John, Willie John McBride, Michael Lynagh and Ian Robertson. An evening to remember, with a lot of seeing and hearing!

The '55 Lions sing again at our Tribute to the Great Cliff Morgan.

Throughout the autumn we had our annual series of Book Launch Lunches/Dinners. Our launch colleagues were a mixture of Willie John McBride, Gavin Hastings, Gareth Chilcott, Gordon Brown, Dr Terry Crystal (the England XV medico and a very funny man) and last but certainly not least the irrepressible Max Boyce – boyo, was he brilliant! Even more brilliant was our MC and joint editor of this tome, Ian Robertson, who not only organised most things relating to the book but also managed at the end of it all to increase Spoon's coffers by around £100,000. A collective number of more than 2,400 attendees meant a lot more seeing and a considerable amount more hearing.

Also in November we held our annual extravaganza, The Spoon Ball. The theme this year was A Winter Wonderland Ball, and it really was dazzling, with special effects of real snow, a fiery grotto and a dancing car (courtesy of Vauxhall Motors) suspended from the ceiling. We even had a motor bike (courtesy of Honda) roaring into life with thunderous effect. A total of 1,128 happy people were present for a panorama of seeing and a crescendo of hearing!

In December we also had another tribute dinner, this time to the Barbarians Rugby Football Club. We were graced by the presence of His Royal Highness, The Prince Edward, who met the surviving members of the first Barbarians rugby match against an international side way back in 1948. We also had the all-conquering Barbarians side of 1973 (yes, that match!) in full attendance. What an evening, what a privilege, and what a delight it was to see those great players again together honouring a very great traditional rugby club. So thank you, Micky Steele-Bodger, the Barbarians President, for coming to see us, and we loved hearing all about the Barbarians and Wooden Spoon!

At the back end of the season we were selected for our first appearance as the benefiting charity at the National Shell UK Schoolboy Seven-a-Side Tournament at Rosslyn Park. This wonderful event, now 60 years old and sponsored over the past few years by Shell UK, was again a privilege for Wooden Spoon Society to be associated with. We provided the prizes for the replay of the initial final between Clifton College and St George's Harpenden all those years ago. Not the same players, mind you, but we did have at least eight of the original players as very important guests on the day. It was remarkable how vivid the memories were that were being recounted. A memorable occasion and a wonderful event, and it is a pleasant prospect to think that Wooden Spoon Society will stay

Above: Max Boyce is back at his very best. Could that be why Wales are winning again?

Left: Our Guest of Honour at the Barbarians Dinner was His Royal Highness The Prince Edward. Pictured here are (l to r) Willie John McBride, HRH, Mike Parker (Dinner Organiser), and Max McHardy (Greater London Spoon Committee Chairman).

Below left: A giant in rugby – Micky Steele-Bodger (seen here signing Cliff's commemorative print) was the prime mover behind our splendid Tribute to the Barbarians Dinner.

Above right: Our Royal Patron 'opens the curtains' on yet another Spoon Project, the Wooden Spoon Building for the ACE Centre in Oxford.
Right: Our 'Enry Cooper opened the Wooden Spoon Wing of the Ridge School near Sevenoaks, Kent.
Below: Willie John and the Belfast Committee hand over the 'down payment' on the Greenwood House Assessment Centre in Belfast.

involved with this event over the years to come.

A nice touch by our England Patrons, the Rugby Football Union, was to present at the RFU Awards Dinner this year the Annual Unsung Hero Award (in this case heroine) to Rose Tanner, who with husband Peter as Joint Chairman has run these wonderful Schoolboy Sevens for a lot more years than either can care to remember. In fact Peter was first involved with frozen hands and a blunt pencil as a schoolboy and has never stopped! An award fully justified and typical of the game of rugby, where many unsung heroes contribute much in total and unrewarded dedication. Spoon's involvement will give us a great chance to be seen and heard by the emerging generation. First impressions count for so much.

Again late in the season of 1998-99, we reunited that remarkable 1974 Lions side to South Africa in The Deloitte & Touche Recall of 99. Over a quite extraordinary five-day period we had dinner with our Royal Patron, HRH The Princess Royal, at Murrayfield Stadium; we had an Irish Craic in Dublin; in Cardiff the might of Wales came to greet the Lions in the grounds of Cardiff Castle; and approaching 1,000 people packed the Hilton Hotel, London, for a formal dinner on the last day of the tour. What a gathering, and what a tour, seen and heard by over 3,000 folk in four countries at six events in five days!

While being seen and heard is very important to a growing charity, of even greater importance is the reason why. Therefore, the most memorable thing about the past year is that it was the first in which we gave away £1 million. The pace and growth of Wooden Spoon Society over the last seven or eight years can only modestly be described as exponential. Over the past 14 months Wooden Spoon Society has funded or part-funded projects to the value of £1.4 million, and over the next 20 months will be responsible for funding or part-funding projects to the value of £4.3 million.

That growth is quite staggering and is a reflection on the enthusiasm and support of our ever-growing membership. Perhaps the most heart-warming aspect is that it shows in a most positive fashion the compassionate face of arguably the finest team game in the world.

Rugby teaches compassion and magnanimity, it teaches respect for the opponent and it teaches appreciation of the efforts of others. These attributes when reflected into society ensure that Wooden Spoon Society as the Charity of British Rugby will go on transferring the goodwill from the game to those less-advantaged youngsters who are most deserving of our thoughts and deeds.

We have been privileged in Wooden Spoon Society to have the support of rugby – generally from our membership and particularly from the figureheads of the game who give their time and energy to help us to create opportunities for others. It is a most rewarding task and the results are there for all to see.

We now approach probably our most momentous season to date. As the World Cup descends upon Cardiff, so the opportunity of becoming a charity that is heard as well as seen becomes manifest. A terrific programme of events has been planned, and as people leave Cardiff after the RWC Final they will reflect upon Wales, a country vibrant with the culture of rugby; the whole British Isles, where the game is loved deeply; a European continent that has made them welcome; and a charity that does much good for children and young people in a society that reflects the game itself.

We now pause and consider that if we have achieved this much when no one seems to have heard of us just imagine how much we will achieve when everyone has seen and heard of Wooden Spoon Society.

For details of membership of Wooden Spoon Society ring/fax/email or write to:

The Spoon Office
35 Maugham Court
Whitstable
Kent CT5 4RR
01227 772295 (tel); 01227 772296 (fax) or
charity@woodenspoonsoc.org.uk

Left: Our Hon. Regional Presidents Rob Andrew (North East Committee) and Bill Beaumont (North West Committee) open the new Lloyds TSB Cashpoint at Twickenham; the first withdrawal was £2,000 to Wooden Spoon. Below: The newly decorated Wooden Spoon Bar at Twickenham (thank you Tetley's) is opened for business by Jason Leonard.

THE REUNION OF THE '74 LIONS

The victorious '74 Lions on their 25th Anniversary Reunion organised by the **Wooden Spoon Society**

Standing rear:
JPR Williams,
Geoff Evans,
Tom Grace,
Mike Gibson,
Merv Davies,
Stuart McKinney,
Clive Rees,
Andy Ripley,
JJ Williams,
Chris Ralston,
Gordon Brown,
Phil Bennett,
Roger Uttley,
Alan Old,
Fran Cotton,
Ian McLauchlan,
Mike Burton,
Dr Ken Kennedy,
Dick Milliken,
Alan Morley,
John Moloney,
Roy Bergiers.
Seated: Andy Irvine,
Gareth Edwards,
Choet Visser,
Willie John McBride,
Dr Syd Millar,
Sandy Carmichael,
Billy Steele,
Tommy David.
Seated on floor:
David Roberts
(Executive Director,
Wooden Spoon
Society),
John Lawrence (Team
Liaison Manager).

Top left: Her Royal Highness The Princess Royal arrives at Murrayfield. L to r: Jules Gammond, Derek Brown (President, SRU), David Roberts (Executive Director, Wooden Spoon Society), Her Royal Highness The Princess Royal, the Right Honourable Lord Provost of Edinburgh. Centre left: A proud Willie John McBride accompanies Her Royal Highness into Murrayfield. Near left: An apt moment at Murrayfield, as we had with us the Five Nations Trophy recently won by Scotland and proudly held by the brothers 'Broon', Gordon and Peter. Bottom left: Our special guests Christa and Hannes Marais (the 1974 Springbok captain) proudly hold the specially commissioned '74 Lions Grogg (still available from the Spoon Office).

Above: In Dublin we had River dancers and a great sponsor in First Active. Top right: As on every tour, you have to do some standing and waiting. Stuart McKinney, Fergus Slattery, Willie John and his best friend the inevitable pipe. Right: Her Royal Highness makes some enquiries about Rugby World Cup final tickets from the irrepressible Mike Burton. Fran Cotton looks pleased at the prices quoted.

The fund-raising success of the Deloitte & Touche Recall of 99 was assured by the additional and enthusiastic support of Beamish, DHL, Famous Grouse, First Active, First Plus, Julian Hodge Bank, McEwans, Tetley's Bitter and Waterford Crystal.

Above: Scottish sponsor Richard Keith of Scottish and Newcastle greets old friends Ian McGeechan and Fergus Slattery. Far left: Gordon Brown and Billy Steele with yet another rendition of the tour song 'Flower of Scotland'. Near left: Garry Richardson was in fine form at the Hilton keeping all in order.

NEXT

Next are pleased to support the
Wooden Spoon Society

THE NEXT CENTURY

Wooden Spoon Society

SUPPORTING TOWN HOUSES, COUNTRY HOUSES & BRICK HOUSES.

Cheltenham & Gloucester

Cheltenham & Gloucester plc   Registered Office   Barnett Way   Gloucester GL4 3RL

A SAD LEGACY FOR THE 21st CENTURY

BY NIGEL STARMER-SMITH

What do you regard as the most disturbing development in rugby? For me it is the fact that lies behind the headlines: I am told that the number of players participating in the game in the UK has dropped in the past two years by something of the order of 20 per cent. The number of clubs has remained fairly constant, but within clubs the number of teams running out on a Saturday has fallen dramatically. Small wonder. I have little sympathy for the famous clubs that are teetering on the brink of financial ruin – or that have actually pressed the self-destruct button. My concern is for those junior clubs which have been the life blood of the game for so long for the vast majority and which now find themselves unable to field more than one team where once they may have had three, four or five. By and large, they are the innocent victims of the trail of disaster of the past three years. Just tour round the Greater London area, for example, and ask in the rugby club houses how many active players remain on the books. Ask the clubs, too, what measure of assistance they have received from their governing body.

I am not surprised at the situation, for had ever a group of persons administering a sport in the British Isles sat down to plot and execute the downfall of their game they could scarcely have made a better job of it than those who have had the reins of responsibility at Union and club level since the first moves towards all-out professionalism in 1995. Here's the formula.

Firstly, you pander to the Unions south of the equator urging full professionalism and to that small clutch of self-interested players with eyes on their pockets alone. For heaven's sake, how many people ever wanted it? Was there ever a referendum among members? Was there a mandate given to anyone, ever, to implement it? Never.

Secondly, you make sure that control of the game, in practical terms, is ceded to a few major clubs – in England that equates to something like one one-hundred-and-fiftieth of

'The number of clubs has remained fairly constant, but within clubs the number of teams running out on a Saturday has fallen dramatically.'

the membership of the Rugby Football Union – by allowing them to own all the leading players through contract. And then you sit back and watch the inevitable transfer of ownership of these clubs, their players and assets – and hence their future well-being – to a handful of individuals scarcely steeped in the game.

Next you make sure that access to the most important vehicle for maintaining a high public profile and wider interest in the game – television – is confined to the smallest possible number of viewers by giving principal transmission rights to satellite channels. Public interest evaporates – and we're talking millions here, not a few extra bums on seats at club games.

Thereafter you succeed in ensuring that the media have a field day – or year – in documenting every unsavoury dispute that is eagerly placed in the public domain. The headlines are invariably bad news as one crisis follows another – the negative impact on the public perception of the sport is tremendous.

As for numbers, there was much less discussion about locating a decent number 10 for England than there was about figures all up in the millions: losses of £1.65 million for Bath, £1.4 million for London Irish, £2.5 million for the RFU; the lottery-scale numbers of Newcastle's write-off and Richmond's loans together with wage caps of £1.8 million for Premiership squads; and debts of over £30 million on Twickenham Stadium. Names ousted from – or was it into – the limelight included John Kingston, Richard Hill, Rob

Former Bath and England scrum half Richard Hill was dismissed by Gloucester, becoming one of a number of English Premiership coaches who lost their jobs.

Smith and John Mitchell – all players of yesteryear, but now English Premiership coaches removed from office. So what is the legacy now for the new Millennium?

Where once we had camaraderie and Corinthian spirit in the changing rooms of famous clubs and good sportsmanship on the field, that has now translated to mental intensity allied to financial motivation, and, in terms of the action, physical impact and confrontation. Where once we had that rewarding mix of member, first-teamer and 'Extra B' man in the club bar, we now have player allocation to hospitality suites, draughty soccer stadium corridor bars with plastic cups, and visiting teams that even come and go in their tracksuits. At the top level, club identities have degenerated into meaningless accumulations of multi-national players. Did you ever expect to see the London Irish XV with just one Irishman in the line-up or a Harlequin selection with two-thirds non-English-qualified players? I'm also sure it's not rose-coloured spectacles that influence my vision in allowing me to believe that the game a decade ago was far less littered with serious injuries to legs, arms and shoulders than it is now.

And by the very nature of the full-time commitment the game requires at the top level, we now have a sport that would have no place for a JPR, a Mike Gibson or an Andy Irvine or anyone with intelligence to follow a worthwhile lifelong career. So I would be grateful if someone would tell me precisely who (apart from a cluster of 'got rich quick' international stars) or what has benefited from the advent of professional club rugby. It is hard to think of one saving grace.

No doubt you'll have read in the press about a rise in playing standards and how this must be beneficial to England's international game. Oh, really! Was the writer watching the same English back division as me this season? Perhaps he was a little confused about nationality when thinking of Tuigamala, Venter, Schuster, Penaud, Pichot, Bachop, Howarth, Mannix, Logan, Bateman, O'Shea, Constable and co. But then aren't something like 60 per cent of all players in the English first division non-England qualified? That's great for English rugby? It doesn't do much for the club game in Scotland, Wales or Ireland either! And as for a sport for all shapes and sizes of men – which was one of its greatest, most important attributes – we're getting even closer to the 'universal player', regardless of position, who needs to be 16 stone plus (without helmet, padding etc.), more than six feet tall, can sprint 100 metres in well under 12 seconds and will be burnt out, or broken, by 26.

So we end the 20th century in England with rugby at its lowest ebb – in a far worse position in my view than where it stood in the 1890s at the time of the Great Schism and Northern breakaway. It's hard to credit the fact that its future seems less secure than it ever has been, when a handful of years ago rugby's star was shining so bright and was still in the ascendant. Alienation of traditional supporters is rampant; disillusionment widespread.

Irish hooker Keith Wood of Harlequins runs into a London Irish defence consisting of former All Black and Western Samoan international Stephen Bachop and South African Brendan Venter.

Is there a solution? Maybe. Firstly, professional rugby must be confined to the international game, and top league rugby restricted to part-time professionalism. When, and if, the RFU manages once again to balance its books (as it succeeded in doing before the game turned pro) all its resources must be invested where the money is most needed: not in propping up the professional club game, where the financial equations will never balance, but in developing the most important elements of the game – the junior clubs and junior age levels. It is, after all, *their* RFU, so much more than that of a handful of clubs who, with a couple of notable exceptions, have been in cloud cuckoo land for the past three years. I can think of more than a few people who should be sued for negligence, for not handling a sport with due care and attention, and worst of all for killing off those qualities that made rugby a world-wide, non-exclusive fellowship, the envy of all other sports. Ave atque vale!

THE WAY AHEAD

BY **VERNON PUGH**

After some turbulent times in recent years, rugby has passed through a crossroads and is moving on in pretty good shape. The real news for the future is that our game is now well on the way to being a global sport. That impetus was started by the concept and organisation of the Rugby World Cup (RWC) Tournament. It progressed with the re-introduction of South Africa into the international rugby family; the revolution in broadcasting technology providing genuine competition and better value for sports rights; a landmark Rugby World Cup Finals in 1995; and the declaration of the open game in August 1995.

The pace of change has been considerable. It has also been characterised by the promotion of varying and sometimes conflicting interests and ambitions. That combination has meant that the direction, ordering and regulation of the changes has not been a straightforward task. Some of the things done have been painful and wrong, but generally the central focus has been retained. Happily, by now, most of these major difficulties are resolved or are on the way to satisfactory resolution.

The rugby world has a wonderfully successful RWC competition. It is commercially strong and a solid source of revenue for future development of the game by the IRB. The major unions in Europe look forward to the new Six Nations, having celebrated the last Five Nations in great style, as one of the best and most exciting in its history. The IRB is funding a second Five Nations Championship to start in February 2000 with Spain, Portugal, Georgia, Netherlands and Romania taking part. An IRB Regional Director of Rugby has been appointed to organise and assist development in Europe, and soon a

Italy's scrum half Alessandro Troncon whips the ball out to his backs during the November 1998 international against England. In 2000 the two countries will clash in the inaugural Six Nations Championship.

John Leslie is stopped in his tracks during the Scotland v Portugal World Cup qualifier in November 1998. Portugal will take part in a new, IRB-funded Five Nations Championship beginning in February 2000, along with Spain, Georgia, Netherlands and Romania.

structured competition for over 30 unions will be put in place. In the Pacific and Americas, at long last a high-quality annual competition has been established, again supported by IRB funds – Fiji, Tonga, Samoa, Japan, the USA and Canada have enjoyed the first Epson Cup. Next year, they will be joined by Argentina, and that competition will fulfil the need to provide quality matches on a regular basis for all the major rugby-playing countries. The Tri-Nations continues to offer a great spectacle and leads the world in quality and excellence.

The structure of the sevens game is being formalised, as the IRB pulls together a series of worldwide venues to host an annual World Rugby sevens Grand Prix, starting in late 1999. This will feature the best of the existing tournaments and the introduction of new locations in a 10–12-venue series running from late November to the end of May. Part of the series will be devoted to a second tier for the developing unions in the geographic region of the host venue. Added to all this is the introduction of rugby into major multi-sports events. The Asian Games in Bangkok had rugby 15s and sevens as medal sports; the African Games in September 1999 will feature 15s as a medal sport; the sevens at the last Commonwealth Games in Kuala Lumpur was an outstanding success, and rugby will feature in the Manchester Games in 2002; rugby will be in the World Games in Japan in 2001; and its return as an Olympic sport is being sought.

Underpinning these competitions is the development programme worldwide, which is being driven on by the IRB as we seek to raise standards in the already competent unions and to promote rugby in those where the sport is still very young. This is expensive and it is not easy to prioritise, but the rewards are very encouraging. All the big unions have now put their weight firmly behind the programme, with the guaranteed availability to developing unions of a selection of coaches, physios, fitness experts and administrators for at least three weeks each year under the direction of the IRB Development Manager.

The whole programme will be interwoven with regional structures providing an administrative, political and development role.

Rugby has had problems in their plenty, generated largely by misjudgement of the place and value of non-international rugby in the overall picture. The inevitability of having to live within the means available and of the need to have that means sustainable is now being acknowledged. The club game in Europe should settle soon into a dynamic, exciting but stable format, as a structured season and an apportioned responsibility for funding the professional game is established.

The Ulster defence descends on Jean-Luc Sadourny of Colomiers during the final of the 1998-99 European Cup. 'The European Cup and Shield will replicate many of the features and the pluses of the Super-12 but with a changing cast of teams.'

The European Cup and Shield will replicate many of the features and the pluses of the Super-12 but with a changing cast of teams based on meritocracy as the strength of particular clubs ebbs and flows. The more volatile elements of the game have settled and are stabilising. The patience shown by the rest of the world as the English, the Welsh and, to a lesser extent, the French sorted out their domestic difficulties has been welcome and greatly appreciated. The professional element of the game is with us to stay, and three or so years after its introduction is now part of the framework. Despite the problems, I suppose most of us would have settled for that when the open game was announced that afternoon in August 1995 in the Hotel Ambassador in Paris.

Rugby is in pretty good shape – it could, of course, be even better. However, when one looks at the problems, selfishness, and declining standards on and off the field in almost all the other major world sports, it is good to be part of a developing and vibrant team game where the decent central values of rugby still form its present and are strong enough to be part of its future.

Wherever we play the game . . .

CLIFFORD CHANCE

200 Aldersgate Street, London EC1A 4JJ
Telephone: 020 7600 1000   Fax: 020 7600 5555
Web: www.cliffordchance.com

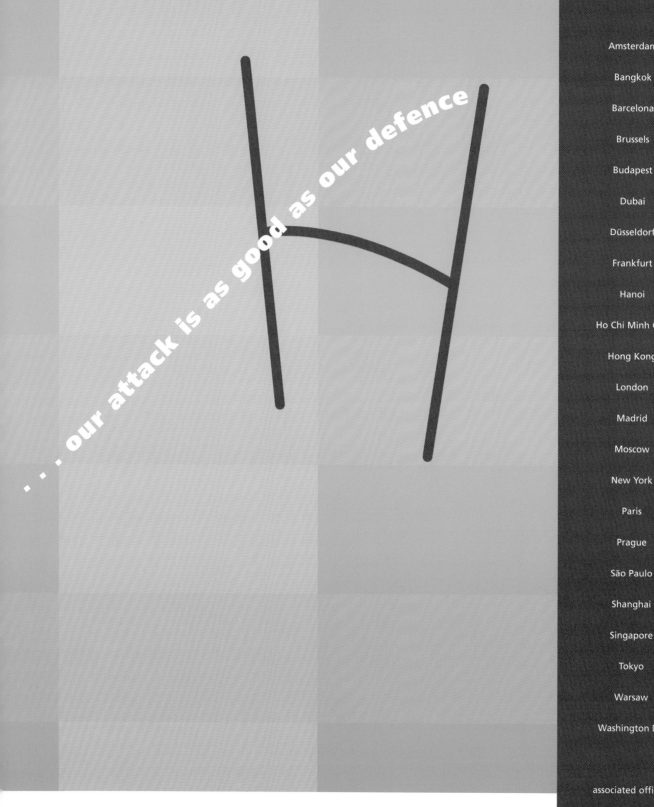

FOR CLUB AND COUNTRY

BY **BRIAN BAISTER**

Playing for their country – Martin Johnson, Jason Leonard and Jeremy Guscott are greeted by England fans as they arrive at Twickenham on international day.

To play for your country remains the dream of every young sportsman and sportswoman, and for an English rugby player nothing epitomises that dream more than representing England in the unique atmosphere of Twickenham Stadium. Is anything more prized than a ticket for an England v Wales fixture, where the spectator rituals before the game are as renowned as the Haka itself? After two years of intensive planning, both sides are finely tuned to outdo the other in singing, drinking, Mexican waves and outrageous outfits – all of which takes place in an atmosphere where the arm of the law is still, thankfully, noticeable by its absence. Not only is international rugby the shop window of our game, but it is a window to rival that of Harrod's or Macy's.

Since the game became professional, the shop window has been enlarged to include England's professional clubs competing in Europe, the Tetley's Bitter Cup, and the Allied Dunbar and Jewson Leagues. All of these competitions are underpinned by the largest number of junior clubs anywhere in the world. The appeal of all these games has spread to a large audience, many of whom will also be among the 74,000 filling Twickenham at an international, the 4.5 million watching on both terrestrial and satellite TV, and the additional 2 million tuning in to BBC Radio 5 Live.

Their attention will be centred on the skills of Martin Johnson and Richard Hill, who first represented England at schools level. Spectators will also admire the Rolls Royce

England flanker Richard Hill in the thick of it against Queensland during the summer 1999 tour of Australia. Hill first represented England at schools level.

speed of Jeremy Guscott and the bulldog tenacity of Jason Leonard, both of whom came through the RFU's youth development system, which is the envy of other sports governing bodies and rugby-playing nations.

But all of the players on the pitch will be primarily under contract not to the RFU but to the leading English clubs, on whom they are dependent for the larger part of their earnings. Having made the point, let me quickly add that as a result of the Mayfair Agreement between the RFU and English Rugby Partnership (i.e. Allied Dunbar League One and Two), there is, in fact, a tri-partite player contract, with the individual player himself being the third party to the contract.

Whether this is the most beneficial arrangement for the game depends largely on whether you sit in the international or club camp. As ever, the RFU finds itself having, of necessity, a foot in both and endeavouring to apply the wisdom of Solomon. Many will now be reaching for their pens (or laptops) and expounding the virtues of the southern hemisphere provincial system, but we must never lose sight of the fact that provincial rugby was largely born of necessity because of the dearth of clubs and a spectator potential that was both small and scattered. England has a club and league structure that is unique both in size and quality, and which, since the advent of professionalism, has acted as a magnet for players from all over the world. The only club system to compare is that of the French, and that is significantly supported and influenced at government level.

Other rugby-playing nations may have a different playing structure and their international players under direct contract. That doesn't necessarily make the northern hemisphere system wrong. We now have well over a hundred years of club rugby, with some 2,500 member clubs, all of whom currently provide an infrastructure to the game that is the envy of the world. To blindly switch to a provincial structure, purely on the basis that it had proved successful in the southern hemisphere, would undoubtedly result in the baby being thrown out with the bath water. On the one hand, we could easily support the old joke about the man who when asked for directions replied, 'Well, if I were you I wouldn't start from here'. On the other hand, it could be argued that the top clubs in England will become provinces in all but name, playing their club rugby in about 10 or 12 centres of population.

What we do have in England is particularly English – evolution not revolution and something that works better the less we try and fix it. What we also have is a degree of partnership and the recognition, by both the Union and the clubs, that strong clubs will benefit the England team and a strong England team can only prove beneficial to the clubs.

The question, therefore, of who should have primacy in an international player's contract needs to be carefully addressed against all of these factors and a background of a recently negotiated three year agreement. It is a fact of life that rugby in England is now a business as well as a game, with both the business and the game being inexorably linked. Any decision has to be based upon the concerns and aspirations of both Club England and the top professional clubs, weighing carefully both the business case and the desire of every English rugby supporter to win the World Cup.

Former England skipper Bill Beaumont chaired the National Playing Committee. He is now the RFU Council's representative at the IRB and on the Six Nations Committee.

Other concerns have also been repeatedly aired by Bill Beaumont's National Playing Committee and the RFU in general. These include:

- More English-qualified players playing at the highest levels in our domestic leagues.
- International touring sides that comprise players who are fully prepared and at the peak of their prowess.
- English international tours put in place with player development and a competitive level playing field in mind, not driven by the sole necessity of fulfilling contractual obligations.
- Increasing the income streams so as to enhance both sustainability and the quality of our top stadiums.

If all of this is to be considered and achieved there must, of necessity, be an even closer partnership between the clubs and the Union, with the right balance of fixtures addressing the complex argument of player burn-out versus club financial viability. Once this is achieved, then, and only then, can we address the question of introducing cross-border competition into our club league structure. But that's a separate argument, perhaps for another day.

Scottish Amicable

Proud sponsors of the
International Rugby
Hall of Fame
Induction Dinner

PRINCIPIS EST VIRTUS MAXIMA, NOSSE SUOS

BY **PAUL STEPHENS**

When Chou En-lai was asked about the long-term consequences of the French Revolution, he replied: 'It's too early to tell.' Given that his answer came some 150 years after the insurgency that led to the overthrow of the French monarchy and the foundation of the First Republic, the questioner was left in no doubt as to how the Chinese like to take their time when considering events that shape the destiny of people.

Those concerned with, and directly affected by, the consequences of the International Rugby Board's decision to permit professionalism do not have the luxury of the time allowed to the then-leader of the Chinese People's Republic, for those consequences are unfolding before our eyes at bewildering speed. In four short years since that momentous ruling in Paris, the game in England – if not in Wales and Scotland, too – has threatened to spiral out of control.

No sooner had another season of turmoil and uncertainty come to a close, and we were preparing to wave goodbye to the England team as they departed on the Cook Cup trip to Australia, than their captain, Lawrence Dallaglio, became the unwitting victim of a cute piece of entrapment journalism. If in the aftermath of this sorry drug-related episode, the members of the Rugby Football Union's Board of Management had submitted themselves for testing, the probability is that in only one or two of them would any positive traces of leadership have been found. No other commodity in the history of the Union is in such short supply at the moment.

It is no coincidence that the game lurches from one crisis to another, or that so many have lost all confidence in those charged with managing its affairs. The RFU are now seen widely to be barely in touch with reality. For certain, they are no longer in touch with the broader constituency of the game. Discontent at the RFU's mismanagement and weak leadership is rampant. If things look bad at Lancaster Gate where, in the space of a few months, the Football Association have dismissed the national coach, Glen Hoddle, accepted the resignation of their chief executive, Graham Kelly, and bade farewell to the chairman, Keith Wiseman, after allegations of various misdemeanours, they are not much better at Twickenham.

After failing to heed the warnings of the International Rugby Board or the Celtic countries for the second time in three years, England were thrown out of the Five Nations Championship. The farce that followed, when after a few pints and some sandwiches in a Glasgow pub they were readmitted, would have been hilarious had it not been for the long-term damage done to England's reputation.

If this wasn't arrogance or incompetence on an unnervingly grand scale by the RFU, then the governing body has been harrowingly inept in conceding far too much ground to the clubs in the Allied Dunbar Premiership, as well as showing excessive leniency in important matters of discipline. Had they not been so, then the leading English clubs would surely have played a substantial part in a vibrant European Cup. Moreover, there would have been no repeat of the misguided clemency shown to Kevin Yates when it came to dealing with Leicester's Austin Healey for stamping on the head of Kevin Putt,

Will things ever look up again for former England skipper Lawrence Dallaglio?

the London Irish scrum half. Instead of treating Healey's foul act with a punishment to fit the crime, there was merely a stern rebuke followed by an inadequate suspension.

Whatever one makes of the Dallaglio imbroglio, it is instructive to contrast the way in which the RFU reacted to the allegations of drug-taking made against him by two tabloid newspapers with the manner in which the Jockey Club handled the Graham Bradley affair. Bradley is a National Hunt jockey who was suspended in April 1999 after allegations of doping and race-fixing were made against him. He, along with five others – including Jamie Osborne, who took a year to clear his name – eventually had their licences restored, although while under investigation they were unable to continue their careers.

On the widespread assumption in English law that someone is innocent until proved guilty, for those involved in this case, their treatment may seem a little harsh. Here, there was an apparent presumption of guilt, right up to the moment when the charges were dropped. Desperate to keep its sport clean, the Jockey Club is not the only organisation to suspend those who are alleged to have committed a wrongdoing, until an inquiry into the case has been completed. Schoolteachers, police officers, most other workers in the public sector, and those in the armed forces have to abide by similar sets of rules. Why not England rugby players?

Racing was once bedevilled by doping, race-fixing and horse-swapping, until the authorities got tough, in a determined attempt to drive the cheats out of their sport. The Jockey Club's senior steward, Christopher Spence, defended the decision to withdraw Bradley's licence pending the outcome of the case. 'When the stewards suspended Bradley's licence, it was stressed that no judgement was being made,' said Spence. 'At all times throughout these investigations, the Jockey Club has sought to uphold public confidence in racing and to protect the integrity of the sport.'

Although no player is bigger than the game, I hope Dallaglio will eventually be proved innocent, which will enable him to emerge completely exonerated, to do what he does best; and that is playing rugby – although I suspect that before he is, he may be obliged to face his accusers in a libel action. The alternative is for us all to accept the findings of the long-delayed RFU inquiry without demur. However, if the suspicion remains that there has been the faintest hint of a cover-up, then the integrity of the RFU could be damaged irreparably.

Brian Baister, the Chairman of the Rugby Football Union's Board of Management. A safe pair of hands, or safely mediocre?

While we are right to be concerned at the outcome of the Dallaglio case and the way the RFU have directed it, there remains the very real problem of diminishing public confidence in the RFU and growing concerns over their competence. The chief executive, Francis Baron, has been a part of the action for only a comparatively short time, so we must mimic Chou En-lai's response when considering his effectiveness. Unfortunately, we cannot be so charitable about the Board of Management as a whole, or in particular its chairman, Brian Baister.

When Baister was elected he was seen as a safe pair of hands. In Westminster parlance, this is usually taken to mean safely mediocre. Nothing Baister has been involved in since he replaced Cliff Brittle suggests otherwise. Baister will be thankful that the Board are no longer threatened by the possibility of a Special General Meeting being called, an event which would almost certainly have brought with it the dangers of a vote of no-confidence. It is very doubtful if they could survive this, although the only reason we

Diminishing numbers at the big games. There is trouble ahead unless the decline in attendances can be arrested.

must be grateful that an SGM is temporarily off the malcontents' agenda is that the blood that would have flowed from it would have been difficult to staunch. Someone must have thought the well-stained Twickenham carpet would be unable to cope if more blood were to be spilt on it.

The disquiet over the RFU's maladroit handling of the Dallaglio issue and their approach to disciplinary matters is perfectly understandable, and the way the RFU have supposedly gone about improving their relationship with the clubs has prompted further alarms and open hostility, for it has been little short of a disaster. Here we are in territory where anarchy rules, without any visible sign of improvement.

It used to be said that if the Church of England was the Tory party at prayer, then if you went into the West Car Park at Twickenham when England were at home, you could witness the Tories at play. These observations were made in the days when England didn't win very often, although they could always be relied upon to manage their affairs with a certainty that was the envy of all other sporting organisations. Not any more.

When private virtue fails – as it allegedly has for Lawrence Dallaglio – we become addicted to it. Elsewhere we are not good at blaming. And I don't just mean in restaurants where poor food and indifferent service warrant censure. We are far too tolerant of organisational failure in Britain, which never seems to lead to personal disgrace.

By not retaining primacy of contract with their international players, and allowing the leading clubs to organise and decide upon the competitions in which they will take part, the RFU have forfeited much of their authority in these key areas. With so little club rugby – and not much live international rugby either – on terrestrial television, the game is denied the valuable exposure it once had. The commercial consequences of the RFU's decision to throw in their lot with Sky, not to mention the consequent reduction in viewing figures, have been a calamity – and this at a time when the sport is desperate to sell itself to a wider audience. But no one seems to care much. No one will be fingered. No one will resign. No one will even be required to answer for the shambles which passes for effective management.

In seeking a wider explanation for this we must turn to the clubs. By allowing them to do almost as they please, the RFU must shoulder most of the blame, though not all of it. In refusing to play in last season's European Cup, the clubs denied themselves additional revenue of £3.5 million. This was no one else's fault but their own. When the season opened, we had fixtures for only the first six weeks as the wrangling over the unnecessary Anglo-Welsh matches grew louder. This was followed by the prolonged arguments over a British league. Soon it became clear there were discontented voices within English First Division Rugby, the body representing the top 14 clubs in the Premiership. Before the season was out, they had turned on two of their own. So Richmond and London Scottish were consigned to their inglorious deaths.

The massive overspending – like the hype, the overblown playing contracts and the unattainable dreams – could only be sustained for so long. Inevitably there had to be casualties as reality replaced the moonshine. One by one the new breed of millionaire investors, who breezed into the game with such extravagant expectations, jumped ship. Frank Warren decided that enough was enough at Bedford. Ashley Levett left the members at Richmond to seek some bereavement counselling, while Sir John Hall departed Newcastle in order to spend more time at his villa in Spain. They are unlikely to be mourned.

Meanwhile, the Premiership One clubs reached the end of the season confronted by an aggregate attendance shortfall of over 15 per cent. In that West Country hotbed Gloucester, gates were down by over 1,500 a match. Before one game at Kingsholm – where admission and season-ticket prices are among the highest in the land – I asked the club owner, Tom Walkinshaw, if falling numbers were not the result of unreasonably high prices. 'I think they probably are,' said Walkinshaw, 'and we shall be doing something about this in the New Year.'

Nothing was done, so many of Gloucester's supporters – surely the most vocal and loyal in England – voted with their feet and stayed away. Even at champions Leicester, gates were down, as they were at Newcastle, who were obliged mid-season to end their ruinously expensive experiment of playing home games at The Gateshead Stadium, because no one wanted to go there. Were any further warnings needed about the clubs taking their supporters for granted, the showpiece Tetley's Bitter Cup final was far from sold out.

For the moment it's all smiles from Francis Baron. But after a troubled first year, the jury is still out on the effectiveness of the RFU's new Chief Executive.

Amid all the wreckage, the RFU stand aloof and alone, as if unable to comprehend how it all came about. The Mayfair Agreement – trumpeted so loudly as the instrument which heralded the end of the disagreements between the Union and the clubs – is neither credible nor verifiable. The members, players and supporters of the smaller clubs, those unpaid volunteers who work so hard to uphold the best traditions of the game they love, feel as if the RFU have broken faith with them. They have been abandoned, their voices unheard.

In his first notable act since becoming chief executive, Francis Baron, confronted by rocketing costs, announced swingeing cuts in the Twickenham budget to stem the losses. His next undertaking should be to remind Brian Baister and the other members of the Board of Management of the Roman poet Marcus Martialis's dictum: *Principis Est Virtus Maxima, nosse suos* – To know his own subjects is the chief duty of a ruler.

THE WORLD'S FAVOURITE TOMATO KETCHUP

RUGBY WORLDWIDE

CATHAY PACIFIC

HOP ON IN THE UK.
HOP OFF IN PERTH,

OR ADELAIDE,

Leap on a Cathay Pacific flight to Hong Kong and hop on to any one of our six Australian destinations. We fly three times a day from the UK – and there are 34 flights a week from Hong Kong to Australia, so you can travel when it best suits you. And of course, you fly in style, pampered by the legendary

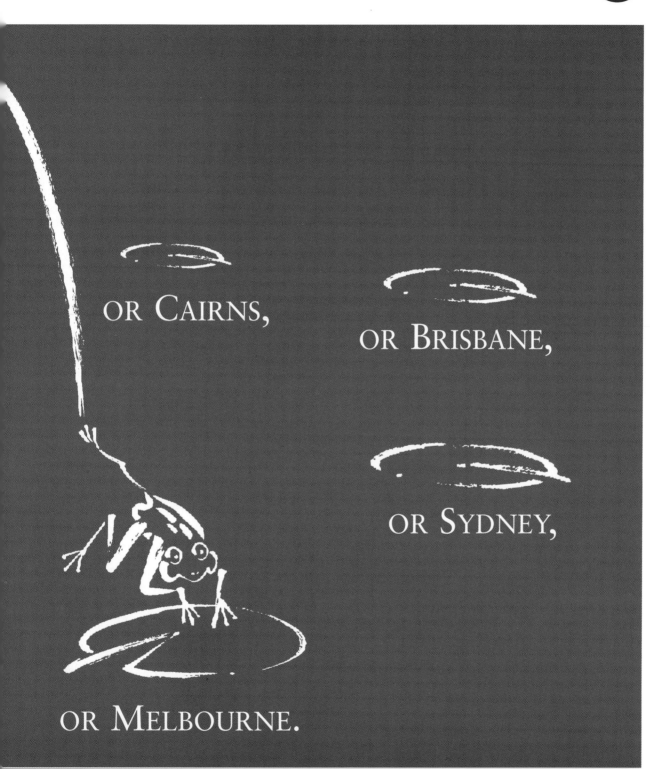

OR CAIRNS,

OR BRISBANE,

OR SYDNEY,

OR MELBOURNE.

SEVENS HEAVEN

BY **ALASTAIR HIGNELL**

South Africa's Joost van der Westhuizen races Fiji's Manasa Bari to the ball during the 1997 World Cup Sevens final in Hong Kong.

The Hong Kong Rugby Union has known about it for years. The Commonwealth Games proved it beyond doubt. Now the International Rugby Board has plugged in to the power of sevens. The IRB's decision to set up a World Rugby Sevens Series – start date December 1999, to be staged over a seven-month period in regional groupings – may prove to be one of the most significant it has ever taken. The response to it – 23 Unions immediately applied to host tournaments in the series – indicates just how highly the shortened game is rated as a means both of attracting new audiences to the sport and of making a tidy profit.

Only Ireland and Wales of the International Board founder-members declined to bid. Surprisingly neither Canada, whose Toronto Skydome made it a very appealing candidate to host the RWC Sevens in 2001, nor the United States applied to be part of the circuit. Otherwise, according to the IRB's Tournaments Manager, Fraser Neill, the quality of submissions from the likes of Dubai and Israel, Japan and Singapore, Kenya and Zimbabwe, Uruguay and Trinidad and Tobago, and even from Yugoslavia was 'extremely high'. Neill further acknowledged that the sheer quantity of the bids means that all the applicants cannot be included in the circuit but hoped nevertheless to include as many as possible by arranging associate satellite tournaments to dovetail into the world series.

Before too long, therefore, the World Sevens Series will be a part of the rugby calendar. Just as in Formula One, athletics and tennis the performers – preceded of course by the television crews, public relations officers, officials and sponsors – will roll into town, strut their stuff at the biggest stadium available, and roll out. The potential is vast; the prospect mouth-watering.

While the IRB is keen to play up the missionary aspect – Neill talks of 'utilising this initial attraction as a stepping-stone to the fifteens game' – rugby fans can enjoy the series as a lavish spectacle in its own right, and those involved in the commercial side can bask in the knowledge that what they have is a televisually magnetic, highly-marketable, sure-fire success.

But who is going to play in it? A world series, in anything but the American interpretation, needs the world to take part. The projected dates for the Sevens Series cut right through the Six Nations Championship in the northern hemisphere and the Super-12 Down Under. If the major Unions were to turn their backs on the new series – as quite scandalously and with far less excuse the European Unions have by and large ignored the Hong Kong tournament for so long – the IRB's initiative would barely get off the ground.

England's support is therefore particularly crucial. Until Fiji took the title at Hong Kong in 1997, England could actually claim to be both official world champions (after Andy Harriman's team of then-unknown youngsters won the inaugural RWC tournament in 1993) and semi-official champions (after a team featuring the likes of Steve Smith, Andy Ripley and Keith Fielding won the Scottish Centenary event, also at Murrayfield, in the 1970s), but both titles were achieved with little in the way of blessing from the RFU.

On to greater things: the 1993 World Cup Sevens proved a launching pad for the careers of several members of this England side, including Lawrence Dallaglio, Nick Beal, Matt Dawson and Tim Rodber.

That has changed. England coach Clive Woodward, no mean sevens player himself, was delighted to stress official support for the abbreviated game when announcing a team to participate in the Air France tournament in Paris in May 1999. 'I am delighted to put sevens back on the agenda. Participation in major sevens tournaments is essential to the development of the national team.' Fully appreciative that the 1993 RWC Sevens campaign had catapulted the likes of Lawrence Dallaglio, Matt Dawson, Nick Beal and Tim Rodber onto the international stage, Woodward had no hesitation in adding, "I look forward to England taking part in all the key tournaments throughout the world, including the Hong Kong event".

If England don't have to look far to see the benefit of sevens to a player's development, neither do Wales. Their captain, Rob Howley, first shot to prominence in the same 1993 tournament. 'I think it is the development of a player. You learn to cope with one-on-one situations. You learn to put players into space and it's crucial in developing the skill factor. I think that every player from the age of 11 or 12 should play sevens rugby. Obviously the intensity increases as you get older. I've been privileged to play sevens at some of the great stadiums like Hong Kong and Dubai and they've taught me how to play the game.'

Howley's enthusiasm for a world series is just as unbridled. 'It will be great. God knows how they'll fit it in, with League and Cup and Six Nations commitments, but I've no doubt it will be something special.'

Timing is of even greater concern to Howley's national coach, Graham Henry. 'Sevens has the potential to develop players who are young and want to go on in the game but I don't think that sevens is what the international fifteen should be involved in. It's been very useful for New Zealand recently as they've concentrated on developing players without having the Test match squad involved and I think that's the right way to go. I wouldn't want my senior players to play sevens. It all depends on strength in depth. There would be no point in flogging players who are trying to play international rugby at Test match level. It would be extremely negative to make them play sevens as well. But if there are youngsters coming on with sufficient ability and they can develop through sevens, then fine.'

The World Sevens Series will therefore have to develop in parallel with the established sequence of Test rugby. The top players, particularly in the northern hemisphere, have neither the energy nor the time to play both. Nobody, realistically, is asking them to. The

The All Blacks squad celebrate after winning the 1996 Hong Kong Sevens. Major sevens tournaments have given a number of All Blacks, including Christian Cullen and Jonah Lomu, the chance to show off their skills to the world. They also give the 'short game' specialists, such as Eric Rush, an opportunity to shine.

new series will of course attract its own specialist practitioners, men like Dallas Seymour and Eric Rush of New Zealand and the incomparable Waisale Serevi of Fiji. More importantly, it will allow the stars of the future to make their mark and develop their skills. Those who have already graduated include All Blacks Jonah Lomu and Christian Cullen, Stephen Larkham of Australia, Joost van der Westhuizen and Bobby Skinstad of South Africa, as well as the aforementioned England stars. Their successors are more than likely to cut their teeth in the new World Series.

Established Unions will gain new stars, developing Unions will gain exposure, the backers will make a killing and the game as a whole will reach new markets. And for the fans? Just a long succession of sevens heavens.

SUPER-12 FINAL 1999

BY RAECHELLE EDWARDS

Driving through the outskirts of Dunedin on 30 May 1999, I mistakenly became part of an overwhelming rugby experience. This was a breeding ground for purists, a population of neighbours united by a single rugby match – the Super-12 final – and the quest for glory. These people would not care one bit if rugby was the only sport in the world. In New Zealand rugby really is a religion!

It was as if their worship had put them in a trance; nothing else mattered. This obsession began to focus in my mind on those windy, tree-lined, green roads, as a mass of blue and yellow balloons and streamers invaded the quiet serenity. I was an impostor – not a South Island New Zealander supporting the Otago Highlanders or the Canterbury Crusaders, merely an Australian on my way to their sacred turf, Carisbrook.

As I came into the centre of town, the frenzy was hitting fever pitch. All of the shops along the main streets of Dunedin – George and Princess – were decorated in the Highlanders' colours, with 'Go Otago' signs everywhere. Even the traffic lights had been changed to blue and yellow! But there was no shortage of red and black either: the Crusaders' fans had arrived in large numbers. Supporters of both sides were running around like crazy people, dressed literally from head to toe in the appropriate shades, sporting dyed hair or bright wigs; countless pairs of shoes had been spray-painted for the occasion. Some of the students weren't wearing much at all, but that didn't stop them from openly displaying which team they were going to be cheering on: body painting was a big hit, in spite of the very cold conditions. Dunedin is a university town, so the students – or 'scarfies', as they are known – packed out the terraces at the ground known the world over as the 'House of Pain'. They arrived with stereos, flags, banners, bottles of vodka and rum – in fact they brought a new meaning to the phrase 'rugby mad'.

The demand for tickets was 80,000, but the capacity at Carisbrook is only 37,000. That didn't stop some temporary seating being erected and 42,000 squishing in for the main event. A lot of body heat from the crowd warmed up the stadium. The game was promoted with a slogan 'Come to the party at Tony Brown's Carisbrook'. This was a send-up of an insurance advertisement which referred to 'Kelly Brown's party' and seemed to capture the imagination of Dunedin. This promotion put a lot of pressure on the Highlanders' fly half, Tony Brown, who was set to challenge Andrew Mehrtens for the All Black number 10 jersey. Ultimately it was the class of Mehrtens that shone through.

Otago winger Brian Lima was the only player to score a try in the first half. Down 6-14 at the break, the Canterbury side threatened to do their familiar Lazarus party trick. They had shown character in the final burst at home before the Super-12 final series, coming back to steal victories after significant half-time deficits against two South African teams, the Cats and the Sharks. Their effort against the Cats, in particular, was superb, Crusaders storming home 58-38 after trailing 31-6. But the Super-12 final is a step up. It is played at a fast and furious pace, and the 1999 match was one of *the* great games of rugby.

Immediately after the break, Crusaders' scrum half Justin Marshall threatened to cross, only to lose the ball over the try line. Two minutes later, Marshall's cousin, centre

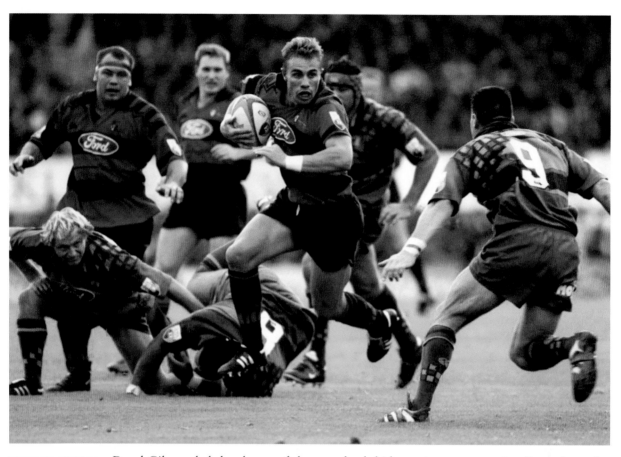

Daryl Gibson, led the charge of the comeback kids, spying a gap to give Canterbury the lead. Then it was up to the man they call 'the Rocket', Afato So'oalo, to chase a perfectly weighted chip-kick down the right wing and beat Jeff Wilson to add five points to the scoreboard and put the icing on the cake for the visitors.

There was a late consolation try for the Highlanders' Isotola Maka but it was irrelevant. The Canterbury Crusaders had won back-to-back Super-12 championships. They defended their title with a 24-19 win. The Crusaders had crashed Tony Brown's party and they were ready to celebrate. What lies at the heart of Canterbury's success is the feeling, spirit and self-belief within the team; they have an unparalleled inclusive mentality. Without getting all warm and fuzzy, the friendships and the enjoyment that the Crusaders share is obvious. 'We do a lot of hard work together, but there is a real equality in the team – no matter how much rugby experience you've had or what you've achieved, you are on the same level as every other guy. The culture of making fun of each other really helps, so that guys don't get too big for their boots,' Andrew Mehrtens said.

When the final whistle was blown I asked a loyal Canterbury supporter, New Zealand Prime Minister Jenny Shippley, for her choice as Man of the Match. She couldn't go past the Crusaders' skipper. 'I'd have to say Todd Blackadder. He has won the heart of Cantabrians; he is an outstanding leader. It was a wonderful game of rugby. I hope that Australians, South Africans and New Zealanders enjoyed the spectacle,' Shippley answered. In reply to this praise the Canterbury captain simply said 'You know the country is in good hands when your leader is wearing red and black'.

Feels familiar. Todd Blackadder, skipper of Canterbury Crusaders, parades the Super-12 trophy for the second year running after his side's 24-19 success over the Otago Highlanders.

BEHIND THE WORLD CUP.

RWC NEWCOMERS

SPAIN – The quest for the Holy Grail

BY CHRIS THAU

Action from Spain's 33-22 victory over Portugal in their RWC European Zone Pool 3 Round B qualifier in Madrid in May 1998. Both sides went through to Pool C in the next stage, where they faced Scotland.

For Spain, reaching the RWC finals was an impossible dream, a genuine achievement on which the fortunes of Spanish rugby are likely to be built. Until this year, the nearest Spain got to a RWC tournament was in 1987, when as a reserve team for the first ever RWC they were on stand-by to replace Fiji, whose participation was uncertain due to a military coup a couple of weeks earlier.

However, the coup leader Colonel Rabaka, while prepared to take on the Fiji establishment and parliament, was not prepared to commit the ultimate profanity in the eyes of this rugby-mad nation – that of denying the Fiji rugby team the right to travel to the RWC in New Zealand. So, with Fiji having duly arrived in Auckland, the Spanish players spent the rest of the 1987 Tournament as interested TV spectators.

After 1987, Spain's nearest sniff of the finals was in the qualifying rounds of the 1991 RWC, when, coached by Frenchman Gérard Murillo, they failed narrowly to secure themselves a place among the last 16. Although deprived of some of their leading players, Spain gave both Italy and Romania, the eventual qualifiers, a torrid time in the final tournament of the European qualifying zone, coming within inches of creating a major upset. An inability to convert pressure into points and a lack of discipline – one of the traditional shortcomings of Spanish rugby – doomed their efforts against the streetwise Italians and Romanians, who nudged their way through to the RWC 1991 finals.

Four years later, in the qualifiers of the 1995 RWC tournament, Spain, coached this time by New Zealander Brice Bevin, failed again in their attempt to reach the elite of the world's game in South Africa. Although they played their hearts out, skipper Jaime Gutierez and his team found themselves at the wrong end of a 50-point defeat at the hands of the rampant Welsh.

'The Spanish team is an image of Spanish rugby and as such it is a melange of its qualities and shortcomings. We play good games and bad games, we produce flashes of magic followed by moments of embarrassment. We have players who could set the world alight one moment to be followed by stunning errors the next; all very much like the Spanish domestic game, which varies between sublime and dismal.' So said Angel Luis Jimenez, the coach of the Spanish team in the early 1980s. The inconsistency at international level, argued the then coach, was a consequence of the ills of the domestic game.

Although Spanish club rugby has made substantial progress in terms of quality, skill and consistency since the 1980s, the overall picture has not changed much. In fact the yawning gap in standards at international level between the aspiring nations and the established forces was cruelly exposed when Spain took on Scotland in the RWC1999 qualifying rounds at Murrayfield last year. Although the Spanish, captained by veteran Alberto Malo, never threw in the towel, they got demolished by the rampant Scots, who admittedly showed early glimpses of the quality and form that won them the Five Nations a few months later. Nevertheless, an increase in numbers of finalists from 16 to 20 and a change in the format of the qualifying process somehow facilitated Spain's third and luckiest attempt to reach the RWC finals. Symbolically, perhaps, for their first-ever appearance on the stage of the world's foremost rugby event, Spain celebrate this year the

Spain's coach Alfonso Feijoo (left) and his captain, the veteran back-row forward Alberto Malo, face the press in Scotland.

70th anninversary of their most celebrated rugby win, a 9-0 defeat of Italy in Barcelona in front of 80,000 spectators. The match, commemorated with a special medal personally presented to the 30 players by the Spanish King Alfonso XIII, was Italy's first ever international.

The 1999 generation is coached by Alfonso Feijoo, a former international centre of repute who played for the World XV in South Africa in the late 1970s. With a team of amateurs, drawn mainly from the amateur Spanish league, Feijoo is aware of the dilemmas facing him and his team. This was clearly expressed in the qualifying tournament in Scotland, when Feijoo's amateurs took on Scotland's professionals. Sadly, very few of the scribes attending the match were prepared to give Spain credit for trying to climb the Everest of rugby, without boots, warm clothes and oxygen masks. This was Spain's first ever adventure into the stratosphere of rugby, and the team came out bruised and battered but with their heads held high. It was only the misguided decision of the Scottish Union to refuse to award caps to their players that soured what should have been a historic occasion for Spanish rugby.

Unlike his Scottish counterparts, and clearly in defiance of the pragmatic trends of the professional game, Feijoo resisted the temptation to bring in the majority of the 20-odd players of Spanish descent identified by his scouts as potential recruits for the national team. In an act of Don Quixotesque defiance he decided to stay loyal to the players who served Spain well in the qualifying rounds, rather than select five or six players of certain international standard to beef up his squad. In José Diaz and Rafael Bastiade, though, Spain's only two 'foreigners' in Edinburgh, Feijoo had – until the unfortunate and perhaps hasty dismissal of Diaz – probably two of his most influential players. Overall there are around two dozen players of Spanish descent, mostly operating in the French league, hovering on the fringes of the side.

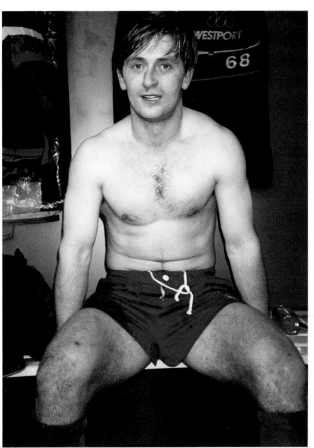

Spain's Ukrainian-born fly half Andrei Kovalenco kicked six penalties in the 21-17 victory over Portugal at Murrayfield in December and followed up with his side's only points – another penalty – against Scotland three days later.

'It would have been easy to select up to a half a dozen players who live and play abroad. And I can assure you that this would have made a difference. I don't think we would have beaten Scotland, but definitely we would have given them a good run for their money. But, rightly or wrongly, I decided to try to qualify with the players who represented Spain in the earlier qualifying rounds, therefore helping to develop our home-based talent. Rugby is developing fast in Spain and the fact that we reached the RWC finals for the first time will help to strengthen our position in the very competitive Spanish sports market. To give you an example, which would have been unthinkable a few years ago: the TV station covering one of the soccer matches involving Real Madrid interrupted the programme to announce that Spain have reached the final of the RWC. For us this would have been unthinkable a few years ago and the RWC success could provide Spanish rugby with a launching pad in the new and exciting professional era.'

In sport, the will to win is based on a number of fundamental and complementary qualities: confidence, teamwork, planning and, perhaps above all, total commitment.

In business, Nokia has long adopted this approach and, as a result, is one of the world's most dynamic and successful telecommunications companies.

Our association with the Wooden Spoon Society is a practical demonstration of our commitment to these common aims.

Strong Connections

NOKIA

CONNECTING PEOPLE

www.nokia.com

URUGUAY – Alive!

BY CHRIS THAU

*O*n October 13, 1972 a charter flight from Montevideo in Uruguay to Santiago in Chile crashed in the Andes mountains. Aboard the doomed flight were 45 passengers – rugby players from the Old Christians club, the youth team of the club, and their families. After a three-month ordeal in the mountains, the 16 survivors were rescued by Chilean mountaineers. The drama, immortalised in an emotional feature film, 'Alive', has marked Uruguayan rugby forever. Chris Thau, who met some of the survivors during his trips to South America, has pieced together the rugby story of this amazing adventure, which somehow may help to understand the 'never say die' mentality of the Uruguay players as they reached the RWC finals for the first time.*

'There is a steel in Uruguayan players which only becomes apparent when they are under pressure. This is expressed in our ability to challenge Argentina when given the resources of Argentine rugby and the shortages of Uruguay – there should be no contest between the two teams. But we have always given them a good game. Although our kids grow up in the comparative comfort of middle and upper class families, they have retained a primeval capacity to adapt to difficult circumstances. I can't quite pin-point the explanation, but when Uruguayans have their backs to the wall they will come out fighting,' said Gustavo Zerbino, one of the heroes of Uruguayan rugby.

Carrasco Polo Club, Montevideo, the home stadium of Uruguay's national rugby team.

Zerbino, a former international player and senior officer of his Union, is probably better qualified than most to explain how Uruguayan youngsters would cope in a difficult situation. The 44-year-old businessman is one of the 16 survivors of the ill-fated flight from Montevideo to Santiago, which crashed in the Andes mountains 27 years ago. More than half of the 45 people on board were rugby players, members of Old Christians Old Boys Club, founded by former pupils of the Christian Brothers College in Montevideo. The rest were their families and supporters.

'After we were rescued, we were told by our seniors that it was impossible to survive in these conditions. Perhaps the fact that we were so naive was a bonus. We didn't know anything about survival in the mountains and that may have saved our lives. Experienced mountaineers argued that no one could survive in such conditions, but, although we were tested to the full, we proved them wrong,' Zerbino said.

'It is difficult to say what kept us alive, other than our unerring faith, our will to live and, of course, God's will. We were just a bunch of teenagers with little or no life experience. But there is very little doubt that the fact that we were former schoolmates, that we trusted each other, that we were committed Christians and that we played rugby together helped,' said Zerbino.

Details of the dramatic story are well publicised: the ordeal, which included the deaths of another ten of the survivors of the crash during a subsequent avalanche; the death of team captain Marcelo Perez, who in the two weeks between the crash and his death emerged as a leader of stature; the agonising decision of some of the survivors to eat human flesh of their dead colleagues and relatives, which ultimately secured their survival, and the refusal of others to break religious and social taboos, which resulted in their deaths. Naturally the events have been scrutinised in depth, while the endless stories of human valour and dilemmas, of desperation, love and hope have been explored in many articles, books and the film 'Alive', a sanitised Hollywood version of the tragedy.

However, a less well-publicised aspect of the drama is the impact the event had on Uruguayan rugby. Virtually every passenger on the doomed aircraft came from the same

Crash survivor Gustavo Zerbino (right) with former Uruguay international centre José-Luis Nicola (left) and former Uruguay flanker Alejandro Nicolich.

Zerbino with Alvaro Mangino. One of the six rugby players who survived the disaster, Alvaro suffered a severe leg injury and had to give up the game.

area – Carrasco, a middle-class neighbourhood of Montevideo. The national ground of Uruguayan rugby is that of Carrasco Polo Rugby Club in the middle of Carrasco itself. There is hardly anybody in Carrasco who did not have at least a relative or a friend on board the doomed aircraft. The accident scarred the soul of the community and of Uruguayan rugby.

Former Uruguay utility back Marcelo Nicola was only five when both his father and mother perished in the crash. Quiet and introverted, he was reluctant to talk about the traumatic events, but his brother José-Luis – one of the great Uruguayan centres of the 1980s – had vivid memories of the tragedy.

'Our father, Francisco Nicola, was not supposed to be on that flight, but the coach of the junior side, Brother O'Donnell, could not go to Chile so he asked my dad to take over. He was very keen to go; he even took his boots with him in the hope that he might get a game. He was a good athlete, a former Uruguay swimming champion and a fine centre threequarter. They still remember him in Chile as the chap who could tackle all their back division one by one, from fly half to the wing. I was 12 when he and my mother, Esther, died in the crash. I tried to give Marcelo the kind of support my father gave me, and that included rugby tuition. I tried very hard. My relationship with my brother was modelled on my relationship with my father. I always said that I had too short a time with my father, but he gave me more in that time than other parents give their children in a lifetime,' José-Luis said.

Alejandro Nicolich, a former international flank forward himself, is the surviving brother of Gustavo, at the time the 18-year-old full back of the Old Christians. Another story of another family scarred forever.

'We never quite accepted that he was dead. During the three months between the crash and the miraculous reappearance of the survivors, I remember talking about him at dinner time as if he was out of town. My father hired a private plane to search the mountains. We approached a fortune teller in the Netherlands who told us that there were survivors of an air crash somewhere in the Andes mountains. We never gave up hope that he would eventually turn up. Our real drama began when they found the survivors and we realised that he was not among them. What was the beginning for the

Uruguay (in blue) take on Chile in the RWC. They beat their arch-rivals 20-14 in Round C of the 1999 competition and finished top of their table. After a tough time in Round D, Uruguay passed through Repechage to qualify for the finals in Pool A, the same group as Scotland, South Africa and Spain.

survivors and their families was the end for the rest of us. Had they been lost forever, we would have still be waiting for him now. I was 15 at the time of the crash. I am 36 now and I know that I spent part of my life in place of my brother. He was a veterinary student. I became a veterinary doctor. He played rugby for the Old Christians. Immediately after the crash I joined the club to make up for my lost brother. To some extent the closely knit rugby family and the strong Christian message of our rugby mission helped us to absorb the pain. During the next 14 years we won the Championship 12 times. We wanted to play and to win for those who died,' Nicolich said.

All these interviews took place some four years ago in the wake of Uruguay's unsuccessful campaign for the 1995 RWC, when they came within a converted try of eliminating the formidable Pumas.

The Sunday after a qualifying game against arch-rivals Chile, Zerbino, his wife and children joined another survivor, Alvaro Mangino, and his family at the picturesque Old Christians clubhouse on the outskirts of Montevideo. It is worth mentioning that the clubhouse and the new ground have been built with the royalties received from the book *Alive*. It was the birthday of Felipe Mangino, an Old Christian stalwart himself, and the families got together to celebrate. Interestingly enough, said Zerbino, survivors and the families tend to get together at every opportunity, not just for the annual gathering on 22 December, the day the Christians found them in the mountains.

'After the tragedy and the miraculous escape, rugby helped us to regain our sanity and a sense of being and purpose,' Zerbino added. 'Only six of the 16 survivors were actually rugby players. Roberto Cannessa, Roy Harley, Fernando (Nando) Parrado, Antonio Visentin and myself recommenced playing in March 1973, less than three months after the accident. Alvaro Mangino, though, had shattered his leg during the crash and never played again.

'The Old Christians were desperately short of players at the time. My brother George, who captained the national side five years earlier, came out of retirement to give us a hand. Another brother, Rafael, who was playing soccer at the time, gave up football to help us. He eventually became a fine rugby player and also represented Uruguay. There was incredible passion. We were training every day and played as if our lives depended on it. We had in the field a team of 15 friends and we played each game as if it was the last game in our lives – in the memory of our lost friends.'

The release of the film 'Alive' a few months earlier had brought dormant memories and emotions back to the surface among the families of those who had died.

'The film has moved our emotions again. Everybody meets everybody in Carrasco. Everybody knows everybody. No matter where you go – supermarket, shops, cinema, at the Club – you will meet a relative of someone who died.' Alvaro's wife, Marguerita Mangino, observed they are not forgotten.

'The film was made in the Rocky Mountains in the US. Some of us, Roberto, Nando, Gustavo, Alvaro, Daniel Fernandez, Carlito Baez, Moncho Saveja and their wives, visited the set. We flew in a helicopter to the place where they actually filmed. There was nothing else but snow and sky, white and blue and this aeroplane wreck in the middle. When we stepped onto the snow I had a weird feeling. I simply froze. I was wearing moon-boots, thermal underwear and a special skiing suit. But I could not move. It was as if the blood had left my limbs suddenly. I cried and cried and cried...

'As far as the survivors are concerned the film did a lot of good. Alvaro had a lot of things locked up in his memory. The film unleashed them. He suddenly started to remember things he had forgotten or wanted to forget. He had lived all this time feeling guilty because he had eaten human flesh, but he never said a word. Now for the first time he spoke about his anguish and guilt. In the film he does not really exist – he is a nobody hobbling along in the background because he had broken his leg during the crash – but the screening of the film helped him and the others tremendously. It was like psychotherapy.'

Gustavo Zerbino concluded, 'I often come to the Christian Brothers College to see the kids playing rugby. Rugby has played a significant part in our survival but became even more important afterwards as we tried to rebuild our lives. The night after we were found, a helicopter hoisted to safety eight of us. I was one of the other eight out with the three Chilean rescuers who had stayed behind. Nobody slept that night. The Chileans were very good people. They said we shouldn't tell people what had happened to us and were really trying to protect us. But we had to tell the truth. We owed that much to our dead friends and families. We were the first human beings prepared to acknowledge that we survived that way. As far as rugby is concerned it acted as a therapy afterwards. We played as if nothing had happened. We tried to make other people and ourselves believe that the future was far more important than what happened in the mountains.'

Gustavo Zerbino and family. 'Rugby has played a significant part in our survival but became even more important afterwards as we tried to rebuild our lives.'

PROFILE OF BOBBY SKINSTAD

BY **RAECHELLE EDWARDS**

Bobby Skinstad gives David Corkery the slip during Western Province's 12-6 victory over Ireland at Cape Town in June 1998.

Bobby Skinstad is everything the modern day sports star should be. He is highly talented, a superb athlete, a dynamic player, has a magnetic personality, enjoys life beyond the field, is a marketing machine, and retains a sharp awareness of his priorities, headlined by his determination to win. And he is motivated by his ability to inspire victory and lead his men to great heights. 'I'm very competitive, I'm actually a bit of a bad loser. I won't be sour but I really hate losing,' he explains.

The youngest captain of all the Super-12 teams, Skinstad, who skippers the Stormers, has the potential to become one of the great leaders in the game. 'As a captain, if you are going to be an inspirational leader, then the 14 other guys should know what they have to do, and, if they see you doing it, then they should be inspired to do it themselves,' said the 22-year-old. 'It's like being an officer in the army in the second world war. If you jump over the trenches the other guys should follow you; if they don't it should be your fault as well,' he continued dramatically.

'If you are a good leader, your character is never going to be in question. The difference is probably the quick decisions on the field, maybe also preparation – being able to prepare the players around you without them realising – I think those are factors that change an average leader into a really good leader,' Skinstad continued. 'I think some leadership qualities come naturally – things like charisma, certain people are born with it; bringing out the best in someone else's character is also a fantastic trait of a leader.'

Despite Skinstad's tender age, his team-mates have the utmost admiration for him. 'He's a year younger than me and we've got a similar attitude and similar views on life, and when it comes to captaincy I enjoy him, he's very relaxed and he sees the positive side and the fun side of rugby. He's not too serious, but he's a very competitive guy and he's a good motivator, and he's got a great knowledge of the game and I respect him as a captain,' commented Robbie Fleck, who plays under Skinstad for the Stormers and with him for South Africa.

Skinstad is eclectic and not only looks to rugby for inspiration. 'François Pienaar brought a team together out of a basically rural South Africa and won a World Cup; his man management was incredible,' Skinstad praised. 'But in history there have been also incredible leaders. For me, a guy like Abraham Lincoln was amazing. He went through 30 years of adversity and then became one of the greatest presidents of the United States, to lead them through their darkest hour. Also Winston Churchill. He rallied a small island plus a handful on the continent to beat an awesome army.'

It is interesting that he has two things in common with Gary Teichmann – they attended the same school, Natal's Hilton College, and they were both born in Zimbabwe. The leading question in the Republic for a long time has been not if but when Skinstad will skipper his country. 'I would love to captain South Africa. I have thought about it often and it would be something I would like as a challenge,' Skinstad said. 'The leadership of a country's national team is difficult to say the least, and I would only do it if I felt that I could do it justice.' he added. And it is precisely that level-headed attitude that makes Robert Brian Skinstad the chosen one for the new millennium.

Skinstad's personality is contagious. To be around him means catching his infectious enthusiasm and passion for what he calls 'the magic of rugby'. He alone inspired sell-out crowds of 50,000 each time the Stormers played at Newlands in the Super-12 tournament in 1999. He appealed to the fans to dress in the team's colours and it worked – Newlands became a cauldron of black. Many of his Springbok team-mates describe him as the most well-known personality in South Africa, other than Nelson Mandela. And speaking of top jobs in the Republic, maybe the brilliant back-rower is closer than we think. Before Skinstad's car accident and subsequent knee injury, his support at Newlands was staggering. A spirited eight-year-old girl propelled 'Bobbymania' in the Cape and offered her services as his campaign manager when she arrived at the rugby armed with a handwritten sign to wave about which read 'Bobby for President'. Nothing could have displayed his popularity better.

It's Skinstad v de Glanville and Guscott at Twickenham in December 1998 as Henry Honiball looks on. Unbelievably, Skinstad had appeared for the first time in a Test starting line-up against Scotland the previous month.

The Springboks celebrate Bobby Skinstad's try against a disconcolate Australia at Ellis Park, Johannesburg, in August 1998. South Africa won the match 29-15 to take the Tri-Nations Tournament.

But Skinstad is not just a happy-go-lucky guy who is renowned for turning football matches. He also possesses a sharp rugby mind and knows the importance of image and understands the benefit in endorsements and supporting the team sponsors. In addition to his association with large corporations, Skinstad has also got the media bug, writing a weekly column for the Cape Times. 'It's good fun. I'm still conservative, so I don't really lash out at all, but I'm getting there slowly. People love reading it because it's an insight into the whole rugby lifestyle. You can tell them the inside and outside and they don't really hold it against you. They actually enjoy it, finding out that you are just human,' he explained.

In another bold move Skinstad became the first rugby player to set up his own website, where members of the public can book the breathtaking loose forward for speaking engagements, read his favourite inspirational quotes or drool over the picture gallery. 'I write a weekly column for the Internet and I do a weekly interview in "Q & A" style. It's just for people to contact me and for me to contact them back, general interest and information for people who like the game, or fans who want to know more about the Super-12 or international rugby.'

Skinstad is only too aware that awesome performances on the paddock translate to success on the other side of the fence. And his long-standing statistic of five tries from his first ten Tests isn't bad for a loose forward, particularly for a player who came off the bench in seven of those clashes. His first run-on Test was against Scotland at Murrayfield in 1998. A few months before this promotion, the blistering back-rower broke Australian hearts and the Wallaby back line at Ellis Park with his perfectly weighted dummy and sleight of hand to secure the Tri-Nations Trophy for the Republic.

Assistant Springbok coach Alan Solomons has been a mentor to Bobby at Western Province, and the litigation lawyer turned coach is well aware of Skinstad's capability. 'As a rugby player, Bobby is an exceptional talent. He is still in the infancy of his career and at 22 years he certainly has the potential to become the greatest rugby player ever,' lauded straight-shooter Solomons. 'From a personal point of view, he is really a fantastic bloke.

He is down to earth, he's humble, he's modest, he comes from a very good family, he's had the privilege of a very good school and he's really a decent sort of man, he's a gentleman,' Solomons continued.

At the centre of all this hype is the charming son of a GP in Durban and an Irish-born mother. At school he was successful in swimming, water polo, basketball and cricket, 'but I always wanted to be really competitive in rugby,' Skinstad offers. He went on pursuing his dream at a well-known rugby nursery, Stellenbosch University, a place where he felt he could really 'test' his ability. Skinstad played in the centre and on the wing as a youngster, and that speed and flair shine through now. So, does he feel that he is the prototype for a new style of attacking back-rower who runs the ball more? 'I'm not sure. I'm probably just a pansy who plays out in the backs much of the time rather than joining in all the tough stuff!' he comments with a smile.

His studies for a Bachelor of Arts degree in English and Psychology are on hold for the time being. 'I wanted to go into advertising and we've got two advertising schools in Cape Town, but you've got to do a hell of a lot of practical time which I can't do while I'm playing rugby, so I thought I'd do a BA and then a conversion to a diploma course in advertising,' Skinstad explains. 'I love that field. I love being around creative people and I love copywriting. I love catchy phrases, tunes, lines. That's where my interest in motivation comes from – quotes and sayings from individuals who have made a difference,' he continues.

He sees life beyond rugby as maintaining a connection to the sport that has brought him fame and fortune. 'I think advertising and taking the game to the people is something that I'm very interested in. The marketing of the general idea of the game and the code itself – I think I would really enjoy to be part of that, but I can only wait and see how that pans out as my career goes on.'

While Skinstad's interests lie in seeking out quotes from people who have made a mark during their lives, for a man of 22 years of age he himself has the potential to develop from being everything the modern-day sports star should be to becoming someone everyone will remember.

Skinstad turns on the power as he tries to burst through the middle for Western Province against Griqualand West in a Currie Cup match at Kimberley.

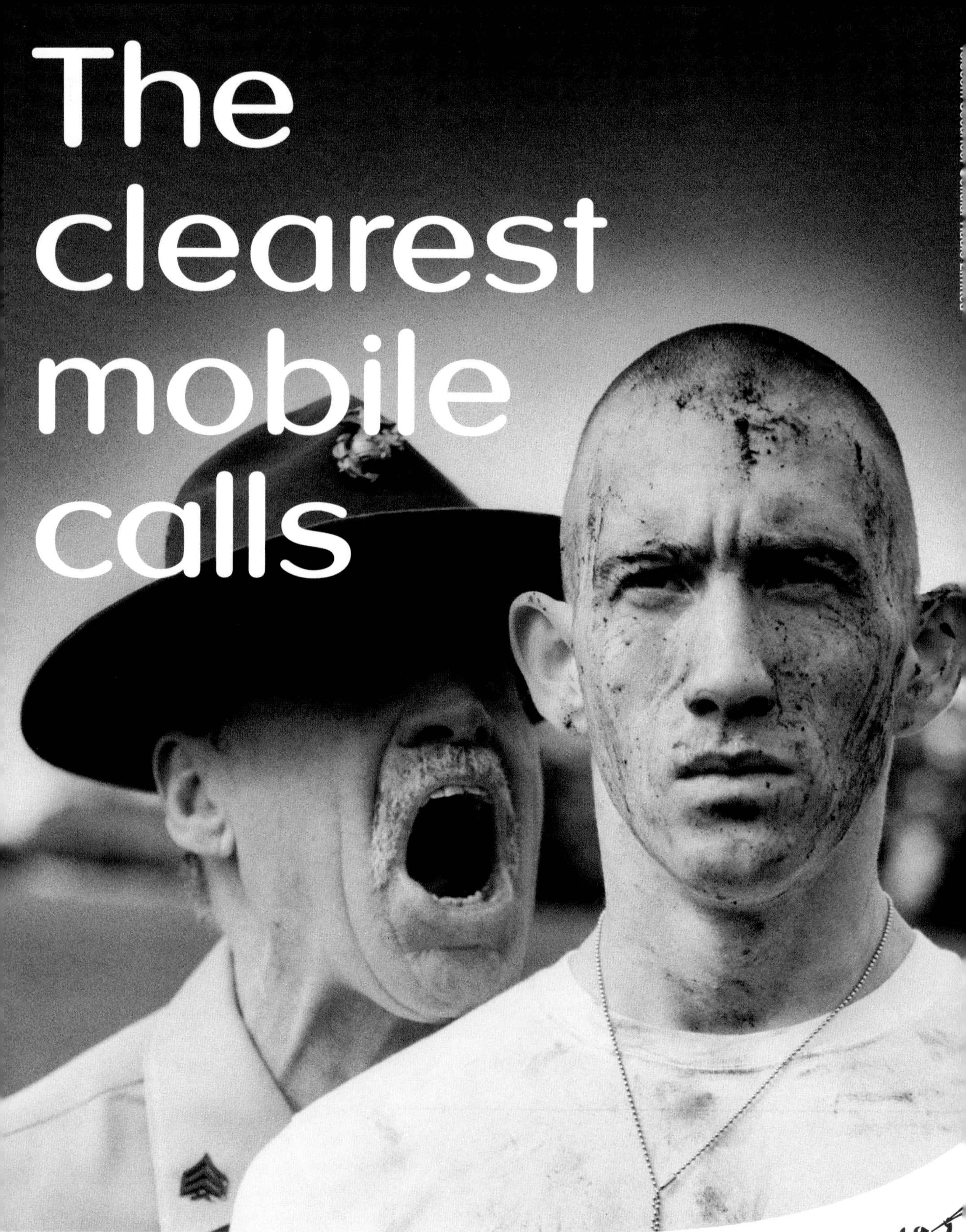

The
clearest
mobile
calls

Call 0800 21 4000

BT Cellnet Clearcall technology reduces background noise on all digital calls.

www.btcellnet.co.uk

BTcellnet
Good cal

SUMMER TOURS

ENGLAND IN AUSTRALIA

BY IAN ROBERTSON

The Centenary Test on 26 June 1999 was much more than a game of international rugby – it was a great occasion. The good folk of Sydney were able to indulge themselves as never before and they took full advantage. It was a glorious opportunity to wallow in nostalgia and take a leisurely stroll down memory lane as the Australians reflected on a hundred years of their heritage, tradition and rugby ethos. It provided excuses for a week-long bacchanalian orgy as, every day for a week, lunches and dinners took place to celebrate all the magical Wallaby moments of the 20th century.

The whole week was brilliantly organised and co-ordinated by the Australian Rugby Union. The England party was left in no doubt that the Wallabies were the stars of the show, and the English players were consigned to the role of extras with not much more than walk-on parts. They attended the main Centenary Dinner and one of the many lunches to hear at both events the highlights of 100 years of Wallaby rugby with hardly a mention of English successes. In one half-hour video presentation the assembled gathering were able to witness the Australians scoring 28 tries, while the sole English piece of the action was restricted to Rob Andrew's dropped goal that gave England victory over Australia in the quarter-final of the 1995 World Cup in Cape Town. This was scarcely an equitable share of the spoils.

Australia's double try scorer Ben Tune clatters into England wing Dan Luger during the Centenary Test at Sydney.

Australian number 12 Nathan Grey lines up a determined Martin Corry. England were 'all fit enough to hop up Everest on one leg backwards'.

But, of course, it was never meant to be that. The celebrations were for the Australian Centenary, not England's, and even that first ever Australian Test on 24 June 1899 was against a British team and not against England. Captained by the Rev Matthew Mullineux, the squad of 21 players comprised 15 from England, three Scots, two Irish and one Welshman. They played 21 matches and lost only three – the First Test, the match against Queensland and a midweek game near the end of the tour against Sydney Metropolitan. They won the Test series by three matches to one and, by all accounts, had the time of their lives. Rev Mullineux dropped himself after the First Test defeat because he felt he was not quite physically robust enough for the rigours and demands of international rugby. At just under 5ft 2ins and weighing only 8½ stones he was probably right. I wonder what he would have made of Jonah Lomu and the modern-day Goliaths who have infiltrated the back divisions as well as the packs at every level of the game nowadays.

The England coach Clive Woodward knew when he landed in Brisbane at the start of his four-week pre-World Cup camp in Australia that history was against an England win in the Centenary Test and he had to put his faith in the law of averages. In all nine previous internationals between the two countries in Australia, the Wallabies had triumphed on every occasion. Furthermore, England had never finished within one score of Australia. In 1998 England had lost by a record margin of 76-0. They were unlikely to be victims of complacency.

From the outset Woodward emphasised that his camp at Couran Cove had one primary object and that was to improve quite dramatically the overall fitness of the entire squad. That objective was achieved. The secondary concern was to win the Centenary Test, but it was underlined throughout the four-week stint that this was unquestionably only the second most important part of the exercise.

The England players confirmed that precious little teamwork was done during the month of June in Australia, and that went a long way to explaining why the players failed to make the most of the chances they created in the Test. They were all fit enough to hop up Everest on one leg backwards, but such conditioning was at the expense of the team's unit skills. Nonetheless, England put up the stiffest of resistance and stretched Australia to the limit in a furiously competitive war of attrition which the Wallabies deserved to win because they outscored England by four tries to two. To their credit, England played their full part in the high profile Centenary Test extravaganza.

The match was the very first Rugby Union game at the magnificent, newly opened Stadium Australia, which will host the 2000 Sydney Olympics. A crowd of 81,000 turned up for the gala event and there was plenty to savour both before and during the game. Preceding the kick-off, the 32 former Wallaby captains were introduced to the crowd.

There followed a procession round the ground of all the great Wallaby teams, with the loudest cheers reserved for Trevor Allan's 1947 heroes and the 1984 Grand Slam side.

There was also another large dollop of Pommie bashing – a favourite Aussie sport – when a motorcade circumnavigated the ground bearing members of the victorious Aussie cricket team who had won the cricket World Cup the previous week. It was made clear to the England side they would be regarded as gold medal Olympic party poopers if they had the temerity to win the Centenary Test.

The English responded mightily. They dominated most of the first half, with Richard Hill in top form in the forwards and both Jonny Wilkinson and Matt Perry outstanding in the backs. Indeed, Perry rounded off an excellent drive by Hill and Tim Rodber to score the first try midway through the half, and Wilkinson converted for a 7-0 lead.

Unfortunately, England kicked away too much possession and failed to score a couple more tries after creating overlaps and gaps. It still looked as if they would finish the half in front, but two vital defensive lapses in the space of four minutes immediately before half-time cost them two tries, both scored by Ben Tune: 10-7 at the interval to Australia.

Eight minutes into the second half and it was 17-7, Joe Roff converting his own try. Midway through the half, Wilkinson kicked a penalty for England, but near the end the Australian captain, David Wilson, crashed over in the corner to ground the ball to the satisfaction of the referee, Colin Hawke, if not to the satisfaction of the England supporters: 22-10 to the Wallabies, and the destiny of the Cook Cup and the Centenary Test had been decided.

The last word, though, belonged to England. In the sixth minute of injury time they launched a final, defiant attack. Phil de Glanville provided a beautifully weighted, deadly accurate, double miss pass which Matt Perry fastened on to, and with the Australian cover defence outflanked he scored his second try of the game. He was my Man of the Match, closely followed by Jonny Wilkinson. These two relatively new kids on the block both have the most exciting futures in the game, and they will surely one day be key men in the first England team to win a Test against the Wallabies in Australia. Despite their efforts, it was not to be in 1999.

England rising star Jonny Wilkinson swerves away from the clutches of Wallaby skipper David Wilson. Wilkinson and Matt Perry were the outstanding England backs in a performance that was a world away from last year's 76-0 drubbing.

IRELAND IN AUSTRALIA

BY IAN ROBERTSON

Former Springbok powerhouse Tiaan Strauss runs in the second of his three tries in the First Test against Ireland, his Test debut for Australia.

The first half of 1999 produced more than its fair share of disappointment for Ireland. They went into the Five Nations Championship full of hope and expectation and they had the bookies running for cover. In the event they managed just one win, against Wales, in four games. They lost to Scotland, England and France and ended the season alongside the French at the bottom of the table. But, if nothing else, the Irish are eternal optimists and they set off on their tour of Australia looking forward to a series of morale-boosting victories less than four months before the World Cup. That is not quite how it turned out. One win over the New South Wales Country XV hardly constituted a successful trip.

The First Test in Brisbane ended in a comprehensive victory for Australia, which was all the more commendable for the Wallabies when you consider it was their first international for over six months and they were missing several key players like John Eales, Steve Larkham and Matt Burke. It was known from the domestic season that the Irish backs lack real cutting edge, with the exception of full back Conor O'Shea, and at the highest level they look a little lightweight. On the other hand the Irish forwards ought to be a match for the best. They have British Lions players in the front row – hooker Keith Wood and tight-head prop Paul Wallace – as well as the vastly experienced Peter

Clohessy. In the engine room of the scrum they have two battle-hardened locks in Paddy Johns and Jeremy Davidson, and it was no surprise they scrummaged well in both Tests.

The line out went reasonably well, but the problems appeared in the back row. Despite their good set-piece effort, they were outplayed in the loose and the back-row combination failed to fire. To their credit, they defended well in the first half. A few tackles were missed, but the whole team covered well and they restricted Australia to just one try, which was scored by Ben Tune.

At half-time Ireland trailed 13-3. Unfortunately, the longer the game went on the more the Wallabies got on top. Kevin Maggs did manage to score one try for Ireland late in the game, but that was their only moment of glory. It was mostly one-way traffic, with the Wallabies running in six more tries for a final margin of 46-10, the highlight being three scores from Tiaan Strauss, the former Springbok playing his first Test for Australia.

In the Second Test in Perth the Irish played a great deal better. Persistent rain made life difficult and the poor conditions suited the Irish. They played with far greater passion and commitment and were swarming all over the Wallabies. They really unsettled them. They led 11-9 at half-time and deservedly increased that to 14-9 early in the second half.

However, their magnificent effort for the first hour took its toll and they faded in the last quarter. The Wallabies took advantage and rattled up 23 points in double-quick time to run out winners by 32-26. The Irish scored two late tries, so they managed to end their tour on a good note. They also unearthed one very promising back for the future – keep an eye out for centre-threequarter Brian O'Driscoll, a player packed with potential.

Wallaby centre Tim Horan scorches through the Irish defence during the Second Test at Perth.

Building teamwork since 1852...

WILLMOTT DIXON

CONSTRUCTION HOUSING PROPERTY SERVICES

www.willmottdixon.co.uk

WALES IN ARGENTINA

BY STEPHEN JONES

It was not entirely a tasteful gesture, although we could forgive it as something that happened in the heat of the moment. But in the second half of the Second Test between Graham Henry's Wales and Argentina, at the Ferro Carril Oeste Stadium in Buenos Aires last June, the Welsh pack drove forward at a scrum and so comprehensively demolished the home eight in what is regarded as the spiritual home and the laboratory of scrummaging that the Puma pack seemed to fold backwards into itself. The scrum ended with the Puma component parts detached and wrecked. It was not long afterwards that Federico Mendez, one of the nobility of world scrummaging, left the field. It was not officially recorded if it was his body or his soul that was hurt.

As that scrum disintegrated, Peter Rogers, the Welsh loose-head prop, gesticulated towards the Argentinians, beckoning them to come for more. Rogers had enjoyed two Test matches in which his authority on the loose-head was comprehensive, every bit as marked as his hegemony over the front rows of France and England in the 1999 Five Nations, and his gesture, an off-the-cuff celebration, was another milestone on the road to the revival so wonderfully plotted by the remarkable Henry. The truth is that around 20 years have passed since there was last any excuse for Wales to be arrogant about anything on the rugby field at any time – and the growing confidence in the Welsh ranks in their five-match run, taking in France, Italy, England and Argentina (twice), was palpable.

Peter Rogers, on the near side, was an especially authoritative figure in a Welsh pack that gave the Puma forwards – no mean scrummagers themselves – a distinctly hard time.

And how big has been the individual contribution of Henry himself? Awesome, to borrow an expression from Down Under. In rugby, we do ascribe far too much importance to the role of the coach, give him too much glory if it all goes well and too much stick if it all goes to pot. But anyone who feels that Henry is coincidental to the Welsh revival is away with the fairies.

Consider the evidence. Henry has precisely the basis on which to work as all the people he succeeded in the Welsh job, none of whom arrested the decline – that is, the abysmal Welsh domestic rugby scene, largely bankrupt, devoid of technical, commercial and marketing inspiration; a ridiculous launch pad from which to strike out for the title. He has largely the same group of players at his disposal. Fair enough, Rogers is a dramatic new force. The giant loose-lead, who idolised Graham Price as a young player, departed for South Africa in his late teens and has returned to the fold – not as the finished article; he has clearly improved since Henry got at him.

Fair enough, too, Henry has access to Shane Howarth, a revelation all season and who was on splendid form in Argentina. Henry has also put together what appears to be a first-class management team of technical, medical and

administrative people, and although it might be unfair to single anyone out, it was obvious to those who followed the team in Argentina that David Pickering, the former Welsh flanker, is an excellent manager; that Lyn Howells, the white-haired, quietly spoken Pontypridd man, is a superb forwards coach; and that Steve Black, the beaming Geordie, is a conditioning coach of quite exceptional talents, as well as a father-confessor for the whole squad. The fact that at the end of the tour, all 37 Welsh players were fit to play was a tribute and – given the Welsh touring history of players dropping like dead flies – a staggering statistic.

But it was Henry who constructed the management team, and apart from Rogers and Howarth the group of players is essentially the same. Yet the effect that Henry has had on individuals hints at a true coaching greatness. Chris Wyatt, catapulting between various clubs, was always a fine talent. Pre-Henry, he won a raft of 'A' caps, but in a country that has been crying out in agony for back-five forwards for so long, he never put up a case to be a top team regular. Henry has done nothing less that grab his talent and turn Wyatt into arguably one of the most important forwards in the Northern Hemisphere. Wyatt's amazing athleticism in the loose and his inch-perfect work in the line out have been a revelation. He was almost perfect in the line out in both Tests against the Pumas and charged around the field to mighty effect.

It is stretching credulity to insist that this is all another coincidence or to be dogmatic and say that the brilliant form of Neil Jenkins is nothing to do with Henry's arrival; or the new maturity of Garin Jenkins at hooker. Or the fact that Scott and Craig Quinnell have put their wilderness years behind them; that Mark Taylor has burst into the forefront of British centres; that Gareth Thomas now finds the old lapses becoming fewer out on his wing. The list goes on, and, of course, whereas Henry has improved the team, its units and its individuals, he has also improved its demeanour. In Argentina, the bitter memories of past Welsh tours, with dire behaviour and dire results, were banished. It took three years after the advent of professionalism for the penny to drop in Wales that professionalism did not simply mean taking money for the poor job you did. It means total dedication, and if Welsh players still have ground to cover, they are on their way.

As Henry keeps on saying, Wales are still an average side – and in true global terms he is perfectly correct. They still have weaknesses. But if average means that they beat France and England, then gain the first ever 2-0 Test series victory by a British Isles side in Argentina, one can only conclude that standards have risen. One year ago, pre-Henry, Welsh followers would have called it glory. Average would have been if they only trailed Romania 10-0 at half-time. Now, it's only average to win five on the trot. For that profound change in stance and perceptions, there is one man to thank.

Statistically, the tour produced three victories from five matches (surely, with a 37-man squad to evaluate, it would not have been too onerous to include one more major provincial match). Wales lost their opening match against

Buenos Aires province and also lost against a very fine Puma 'A' XV in Rosario. The Argentinians were formidably wound up for this match and won a deserved victory, one that exposed the fact that the reserve strength in the Welsh camp is not quite what it could be in all positions – although ironically, it was the Puma 'A' victory that persuaded the selectors to choose Felipe Contepomi for the Second Test against Wales, and the poor

Above: Rhodri Jones touches down during Wales' midweek defeat against Puma 'A' in Rosario.
Left: Gareth Thomas, whose try close to half-time in the First Test helped bring Wales back into the match after they conceded a 23-point deficit.

man endured a nightmare with his kicking and general play. Wales managed to beat Tucuman in the other up-country game.

Both Tests were gladiatorial and exciting, although, to be frank, not of sublime quality, and neither side performed well in the field of continuity. Wales missed the presence of Scott Gibbs in midfield and so were unable to build on the power of their scrum and the splendid Wyatt's work in the line out. Argentina struggled for a forward base. However, they started the First Test explosively, and I suppose that anyone ascribing a little too much power to the Henry magic might conclude that it was all part of his grand plan that Wales should be trailing by 23-0 after 33 minutes of the match. Others might conclude that it was a ruddy awful start.

Argentina scored tries after 24 and 28 minutes. Mendez sent Gonzalo Quesada through for a try to seal a lightning Argentina counterattack, then Octavio Bartolucci, the strapping Argentinian right wing, scored in the corner, after Wales, criminally, had lost control of the ball as they drove it out of defence. Basic ball retention was simply not good enough on tour. A few kicks from Quesada and it was 23-0.

However, Wales scored ten priceless points in the last five minutes of the first half. Jenkins, in his first game since the Wembley triumph, drilled over a penalty, and with Wales at last beginning to move well, a break by Allan Bateman and quick handling by Craig Quinnell and Jenkins put Dafydd James over in the corner. A beautiful conversion from Jenkins sent Wales into the break with hope.

The second half was a different story because tries by Brett Sinkinson, after a clever line-out peel, and another by Wyatt turned the course of the match and Wales won 36-26. It was, according to statisticians, the biggest comeback in a major Test match. Yet there was only one winner throughout the second half.

It was expected that the Pumas would hurl everything into an attempt to reassert their old scrummage domination as the teams returned to the rather ramshackle but rather endearing Ferro Carril Oeste Stadium for the Second Test. All week long, Mendez and his mates had complained of Welsh scrummage tactics. The Second Test was even more fractured, with the whistle of Chris White, the English referee, sounding a concerto.

But the Pumas' power surge was thrown back in their faces. With Rogers and his front row in complete command, the Pumas threatened to disintegrate, and it was a black mark against Wales that they could win only by 23-16. Garin Jenkins scored a try early on after Diego Albanese had struck a clearance kick straight into the midriff of Bateman and the Welsh centre somehow clung on to the ball. Yet Wales trailed 9-8 at half-time and had surrendered the initiative. A long and disgraceful brawl centred around Mauricio Reggiardo, the home prop, and which involved around 20 players, seemed to galvanise Argentina either side of half-time.

However, Wales showed true grit and courage in facing down the dangers; they showed the new confidence that Henry has instilled. The Welsh forward power put Argentina under increasing pressure, and Jenkins kicked Wales away to 23-9 with four more penalties. There was a hairy end-game after Jose Orengo, the home centre, ran in a try after a rare burst of Puma continuity, but Wales held on. The celebrations at the end were heart-felt. They had made hard work of it, but if you examine rugby history you will find that there is no such thing as a bad Test series win in Argentina. It was another step on the long road to world respectability.

Henry returned home with a wonderful job done and, dauntingly, a massive task still ahead. He has impressed many cynics with his quietly persuasive personality, his attention to detail, his all-embracing knowledge of the game. He has also endeared himself with a dust-dry Kiwi wit. He has made rugby bricks with straw and given Wales what is, as yet, an outside chance of reaching the semi-finals of the World Cup. When he began, you could have invested on them losing all their matches. It is a profound transformation, and Argentina was a proving ground of inestimable value.

Wales celebrate their historic Test series win over the Pumas – the first ever 2-0 series victory by a British Isles side in Argentina.

BIGGER AND BETTER: the European Rugby Cup 1999-2000

The European Rugby Cup will be bigger than ever before when it kicks off in November this year, with 24 teams from six countries taking part in the fifth tournament. There will be a wonderful opening weekend when the 1998 winners, Bath, host the inaugural victors, Toulouse, in an ex-Champions' Challenge on 19/21 November.

'The first weekend of next season's European Rugby Cup promises a feast of rugby with great games in each of the six participating countries,' said the newly appointed chairman of European Rugby Cup Ltd, Jean-Pierre Lux.

'It is great news for the leading club and provincial-based competition in the northern hemisphere that teams from all six countries will once more participate in the cup. With the European clubs reunited, the competition will be stronger than ever before.

'The competition will not only be strong in the European Rugby Cup, however, but also in the European Shield. There will be 28 teams from eight countries taking part. Eight have played in the European Rugby Cup before.

'Included in the Shield next season will be last season's European Rugby Cup semi-finalists Perpignan; the 1997 winners and 1998 runners-up, Brive; the 1998 English champions, Newcastle; and two of the qualifying teams for the 1999 Rugby World Cup finals, Spain and Portugal.'

Joining Bath and Toulouse in Pool 2 of the European Rugby Cup are the Welsh Challenge Cup winners, Swansea, and the Italian side Padova, while the reigning

Spain make their debut in the European Shield in 1999-2000. They will hope to have more joy against Biarritz, Bridgend and Gloucester than they did against Scotland in December 1998, when they went down 85-3.

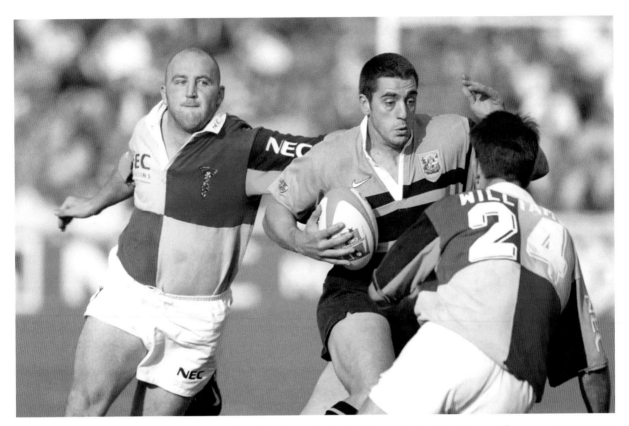

champions, Ulster, face an away trip when they launch their defence in Pool 3. They will meet the French club Bourgoin, who were runners-up in the European Shield and the French Cup finals last season and reached the semi-finals of the French Championship.

The big kick-off in Pool 3 also features a battle between the English Cup winners, Wasps, and the Welsh double winners, Llanelli. Last season's European Rugby Cup runners-up, Colomiers, will face tournament debutants Saracens on the opening weekend. They both figure in Pool 4, which also features the Irish champions, Munster, and Pontypridd.

The English champions, Leicester, who reached the final in 1997, will have to make their third trip to Dublin for their opening match when they tackle Leinster. They won 27-10 on their first visit in 1996, but were beaten 16-9 in front of a packed house of 10,000 people at Donnybrook a year later. Glasgow Caledonians and French Cup winners Stade Français join them in Pool 1.

The European Shield winners Montferrand will travel to face Italian champions Benetton Treviso on their European Rugby Cup debut. At the same time in Pool 5, age-old rivals Cardiff and Harlequins will do battle at Cardiff. Grenoble and Northampton are two more newcomers to the European Rugby Cup in Pool 6. Northampton kick off with a home game against Neath, while Grenoble travel to face Edinburgh Reivers.

In the European Shield, France will have ten teams, England six, Wales five, Italy three, and there will be one each from Ireland, Romania, Spain and Portugal. On the opening weekend Dax host Bristol, Bedford tackle Newport, and Bridgend host Spain. Brive have to travel to London Irish, while Narbonne have home advantage over Newcastle in another plum Anglo-French match.

Harlequins' Keith Wood reaches out for Cardiff's Simon Hill during the clubs' 1997-98 European Cup meeting in London, which Cardiff won 32-31. Cardiff and 'Quins face each other in the Welsh capital in this year's European Shield.

TOGETHER WE CAN BUILD A BETTER FUTURE

We are proud to support the Wooden Spoon Society

www.pwcglobal.com

THE EUROPEAN RUGBY CUP POOLS 1999-2000

EUROPEAN CUP

POOL 1
GLASGOW
CALEDONIANS
LEICESTER
LEINSTER
STADE FRANCAIS

POOL 2
BATH
PADOVA
SWANSEA
TOULOUSE

POOL 3
BOURGOIN
LLANELLI
ULSTER
WASPS

POOL 4
COLOMIERS
MUNSTER
PONTYPRIDD
SARACENS

POOL 5
CARDIFF
HARLEQUINS
MONTFERRAND
TREVISO

POOL 6
EDINBURGH
REIVERS
GRENOBLE
NEATH
NORTHAMPTON

EUROPEAN SHIELD

POOL 1
BEGLES-
        BORDEAUX
BRISTOL
CALVISANO
DAX

POOL 2
BEDFORD
CASTRES
ROVIGO
NEWPORT

POOL 3
CAERPHILLY
PAU
PERPIGNAN
SALE

POOL 4
CONNACHT

EBBW VALE
STEAUA
        BUCHAREST
TOULON

POOL 5
BIARRITZ
BRIDGEND
GLOUCESTER
SPAIN

POOL 6
DUNVANT
NARBONNE
NEWCASTLE
PORTUGAL

POOL 7
AGEN
BRIVE
LONDON IRISH
ROMA

THE EUROPEAN RUGBY CUP 1995 TO DATE

EUROPEAN CUP

1995-96: 12 teams, 15 games, 4 pools of 3, 5 countries.
Final: Toulouse 21, Cardiff 18
(Cardiff Arms Park – 21,800)

1996-97: 20 teams, 47 games, 4 pools of 5, 6 countries.
Final: Brive 28, Leicester 9
(Cardiff Arms Park – 41,664)

1997-98: 20 teams, 70 games, 5 pools of 4, 6 countries.
Final: Bath 19, Brive 18
(Stade Lescure, Bordeaux – 36,500)

1998-99: 16 teams, 55 games, 4 pools of 4, 5 countries.
Final: Ulster 21, Colomiers 6
(Lansdowne Road, Dublin – 49,000)

1999-2000: 24 teams, 79 games, 6 pools of 4, 6 countries.

EUROPEAN SHIELD

1995-96: No competition

1996-97: 24 teams, 67 games, 4 pools of 6, 7 countries.
Final: Bourgoin 18, Castres 9 (Stade de la Méditerranée, Béziers – 10,000)

1997-98: 32 teams, 103 games, 8 Pools of 4, 7 countries.
Final: Colomiers 43, Agen 5
(Les Sept Deniers, Toulouse – 12,500)

1998-99: 21 teams, 70 games, 3 pools of 7. 7 countries.
Final: Montferrand 35, Bourgoin 16
(Stade Gerland, Lyon – 32,700)

1999-2000: 28 teams, 91 games, 7 pools of 4, 8 countries.

A jubilant Ulster team celebrate their 21-6 1998-99 European Cup final victory over French club Colomiers at Lansdowne Road.

NEXT

Next are pleased to support the
Wooden Spoon Society

THE HOME SCENE

YEAR OF THE TIGER: Leicester 1998-99

BY **STUART FARMER**

Tigers' and England skipper Martin Johnson raises aloft the Allied Dunbar Premiership trophy to celebrate the culmination of the Year of the Tiger.

The Chinese Year of the Tiger began on 28 January 1998, and how profound our eastern friends continue to be – by the end of the Chinese year, on 15 February 1999, Leicester Tigers were six points clear in the race for the Premiership with just seven games left!

So much had happened in that year. At the start Dean Richards was still a player with no thoughts whatsoever of managing the team, Australian Bob Dwyer was at the helm, and Tigers had just been knocked out of the Tetley's Bitter Cup. The club had also gone out of the European Cup at the quarter-final stage in November when beaten by Pau in the South of France, and were lying in third place in the Premiership with no prospect of the championship. The Leicester board called for drastic measures – Dwyer's contract, which was due to run out in June, was not renewed, and Leicester's favourite son, Dean Richards, was appointed as team manager. Many eyebrows were raised, not least among the press, where Stuart Barnes, commenting in *The Daily Telegraph* on Tigers' 16-5 loss to Bath at the Rec less than a month after Deano had taken over, wrote, 'The Australian [Dwyer] did not have them in rugby's fast lane, but at least they were on the motorway. Against Bath the impression was of a juggernaut wedged in a country lane.'

Dean's first action as manager was to appoint friend, confidant and back-row ally John Wells as forwards coach, and Springbok World Cup winning fly half Joel Stransky to look after the backs. It was this axis that planned for their assault on the 1998–99 crown. A summer training camp was arranged at Annecy in the French Alps, and on the recruitment front there were three new faces, all of considerable international pedigree – Wallaby Pat Howard from the ACT Brumbies, Tim Stimpson from Newcastle Falcons and burly Canadian wing Dave Lougheed.

The league season began against Harlequins at Welford Road on 5 September, with Leicester ditching their traditional lettering system for more conformist numbers. 'Quins themselves sported a new look in the guise of All Black superstar Zinzan Brooke as player-coach. The Londoners were simply blown away in a seven-try-to-nil, 49-15 battering, and Tigers showed they had really hit the ground running. By the time they had disposed of London Scottish, Northampton and Bedford on the following three Saturdays, Leicester were riding high at the top of the Premiership pile.

As much as anything it was the manner of those victories that was so gratifying. Leicester had won their previous league title in 1995 with powerpack, forward-orientated rugby in which they were led by then-skipper Richards and his back-row mate Wells. It may not have been pretty but, boy, was it effective! The Tigers faithful loved it and justified it all by saying, 'If you've got the best pack in the league then why not use it?' The school of 1998–99 seemed to have once more potentially the best pack in the league but this time had added a top-quality back line to the equation. Full back Stimpson started the season in a blaze of glory and was simply devastating against Northampton. Wings Leon Lloyd and Nigerian-born Nnamdi Ezulike, both locally-produced talent, were red hot, with Ezulike tying the Tigers' record with tries in those four successive league outings. The centres were Stuart Potter, recently capped and a veteran of the previous league-winning campaign, and new boy Pat Howard, who added an extra dimension with his mazy running. The half-back pairing was Austin Healey, now permanently restored to the number 9 jersey, and Joel Stransky, who moulded the lot together and ran the show from fly half.

Another major factor in Tigers' previous championship had been a miserly defence that was the envy of the league. In a further masterstroke Dean Richards recruited the help of Rugby League maestro Phil Larder to assist with defensive strategy. Larder

Above: Dean Richards – from player to Premiership-winning team manager in a little over a year.
Left: Fly half and backs coach Joel Stransky on the break, watched by Tigers colleagues Pat Howard and Austin Healey (on ground).

Wing Nnamdi Ezulike scored tries in four successive matches at the start of the season to tie the Tigers' record.

worked tirelessly to coach the players how to defend as a team in zones rather than as 15 individuals. It seemed that the Leicestershire County Cricket Club's motto of 'There is no "I" in team', which had guided the county to the championship in the summer, had been adopted word for word by the Tigers.

What turned out to be the only blip of the entire league campaign came in October with losses in successive away games at Saracens and London Irish, but by 1 November a 45-15 victory over West Hartlepool at Victoria Park had put Leicester back on the top of the table, and they were never caught. That was despite a third league loss at Wasps in November, when, due to the Mayfair Agreement, Allied Dunbar fixtures were arranged to coincide with England's World Cup qualifying matches against the Netherlands and Italy. Shorn of eight players on England duty, Leicester went down 45-17, conceding almost a sixth of the total number of league tries they were to let in during the entire season! They would go on to lose just once more in the Premiership – at Bath in April – and eventually finish the season with a six-point winning margin in the race for the title.

In was certainly not all plain sailing, though. The coaching triumvirate had to constantly shuffle their resources – especially in the centre, where in the 26 Premiership games they were forced through injuries to change the partnership on 11 occasions, testing seven centre combinations made up of six different players. Will Greenwood made just five appearances, and Stuart Potter missed two months prior to Christmas then didn't play again after January. Joel Stransky picked up knee-ligament damage in the friendly with Fiji in December and never fully recovered, while Pat Howard, alternating between centre and fly half as Stransky's knee injury worsened, picked up a fractured jaw at London Irish and a thigh strain over the New Year.

Involvement in the Tetley's Bitter Cup ended with the quarter-final at Reading's Madejski Stadium, the whole match turning when Tigers' skipper Martin Johnson was sin-binned for deliberately knocking the ball out of scrum half Pichot's hands. TV replays clearly showed that Johnson had legally hacked the ball on; referee Steve Lander and an RFU disciplinary hearing later agreed, and Johnson's white card was struck from the record – but the damage had been done. While Martin was off the field, Richmond scored both their tries and a dozen of the 15 points they managed all afternoon. Credit where credit's due – Richmond's defence took on the iron-curtain quality that had been Leicester's trademark all season, and despite a severe battering over a frantic last 20 minutes, it was breached only in the 72nd minute, but Stimpson's conversion attempt to tie the scores hit the upright.

With the cup and the Five Nations Championship out of the way, the Tigers were able to concentrate on their push for glory, but with Northampton still snapping at their heels Leicester needed to remain focused on their goal. In May Tigers were crowned the 1998–99 Allied Dunbar Premiership champions. Who knows what is in store for World Cup year? Will the Tigers ever-increasing number of current England internationals hit the club hard while the league is played before and during the World Cup itself? Will Leicester conquer Europe? Will it be another year of the Tiger in the Millennium season? It will be great fun finding out.

Neil Back, one of Leicester's large group of England players, gives the Northampton defence the slip during the Tigers' early-season 35-25 Premiership victory.

The Tigers let off steam as Premiership champions after their 72-37 win over West Hartlepool at Welford Road on 16 May 1999.

Property Consultants

Leading the Field
Throughout the Midlands

16 Warwick Row
Coventry CV1 1EJ
Tel: 024 7655 5180
Fax: 024 7622 3434
Email: d&p@holtcommercial.co.uk

THE HENLEY STORY

BY **NIGEL DUDDING**

I had never experienced such scenes of euphoria, emotion and delight as those that greeted the 1st XV as they entered the clubhouse after the game versus Liverpool St Helens on Easter Saturday. The reason? Henley had just defeated one of the oldest clubs in the country, a club steeped in history; Newbury had taken Manchester's enviable home record and consequently Henley were champions of Jewson National League I and therefore promoted to the Allied Dunbar Premiership. There were the old members whom I have known throughout my 20-odd years' association with the club who were moved to tears as they recalled the time when Henley first won the Oxfordshire Cup way back in '79.

So how has this club in a small town of approximately 10,000 inhabitants better known for its Pimms and dress code in the Stewards' Enclosure over the world famous Regatta week rocketed into the so-called big time? There's no financial backer – indeed sponsorship comes in small amounts; there are certainly no multi-national corporations in Henley willing to put in place six-figure deals. Well, while I had the privilege to coach such a talented and committed group of players, we prided ourselves on preparation and team spirit. Abraham Lincoln's famous phrase always springs to mind: 'By failing to prepare you are preparing to fail'. This and many other catchphrases were contained in the players booklet issued to them at the beginning of last season.

So how did it all begin? Henley rugby club was founded in August 1930 as Old Henleinesians RFC. When hostilities broke out in 1939 the ground, Dry Leas, was used for military purposes. Then in 1954 a young Tony Hobbs – who was president 1991–1997 – along with a band of enthusiastic youngsters again established a regular fixture list. In 1963 the name was changed to Henley RFC.

The Henley front row of Lehner, Cassidy and Fuller prepare to pack down against Premiership One club Bedford in the 1998-99 Tetley's Bitter Cup.

WOODEN SPOON SOCIETY RUGBY WORLD '00

Eventually the Oxfordshire Cup was won in 1979, and again in 1983 and 1985. Then with the advent of the Courage leagues Henley were placed in South West Division 2, five leagues below their current status. Everything ticked along quite nicely for a few years, until the publicised arrival on the scene of a new coach – Clive Woodward had been persuaded to start his coaching career at this lowly club, for which he still holds great affection. Clive gave the club's favoured open rugby game a new dimension with the 'flat ball' philosophy he'd seen working so successfully in Australia. The players adapted to this philosophy and to a more disciplined approach to preparation, eventually gaining promotion to South West 1 in 1992, which was quickly followed by elevation to the national leagues in 1994 with a 100 per cent record. Clive departed to higher levels with London Irish five years ago. However, I had the privilege to work alongside him as the forwards coach (there was no room in Clive's new scheme of things for a 'knackered' old forward from the good old days).

In 1995 the club decided the time was right to venture on to a far more effective business footing, while at the same time retaining the family atmosphere. A full-time Director of Rugby, Tony MacArthur, was employed to 'manage the change', and a marketing position was filled to accelerate the club forward. With the Premiership clubs deciding on a 14-team make-up last season and with Henley runners-up in Jewson 2 South, the club gained a further promotion into Jewson National League 1.

The now-famous season started disastrously with a home defeat to Harrogate, but the remarkable team spirit and preparation detail was about to 'kick off'. By Christmas it was clear that the Premiership beckoned; cool heads were needed. I decided to rest four key individuals for the Bedford cup tie in January – the league had to be our priority – but

Henley's Rob Walker (in white) struggles to break free against Richmond.

the eventual victory in that match was truly remarkable. To beat a Premiership 1 side on their own ground will live in memories for many years to come.

Henley's success has always been founded on strong teams, both on and off the field. The ambition for success and promotion has to be wanted by all sections of the club, and this sense of togetherness and collective ambition is shown clearly in our bi-monthly publication *The Hack*. It covers every area of the club from the mini section to the 1st XV, reporting on how the club is achieving at every level. The attractive style in which Henley play has been laid down for a number of years. It helps to draw new players to the club, but they also have to fit in with the ambience – there is still the good old fashioned 'crack' for which rugby clubs are famous.

The Bedford victory was followed by a match at Kingsholm in front of 5,000 people. The day was a memorable one. Many teams from the past re-visited under the new banner of success, and a new name, the 'Hawks' – though not all were totally convinced of the need for this kind of change! Henley's success was also recognised by the world famous Barbarians, who drew on three Henley players (Mark Venner, Peter Davies and Trevor Walsh), recognition not only of the club's status but also of its style of play. Promotion was secured at home against Wharfedale and then the championship on that unforgettable afternoon at Easter.

Other ingredients of success? The best defensive record in the league with an average of only 11.5 points conceded per game. And a willingness to take calculated risks – on and off the field. The future? Who knows? The one thing I do know, though, is that Henley are not just going to sample the Premiership – presumably if you enter a competition of any sort you want to win it!!

KINGSHOLM'S CUP: the Cheltenham & Gloucester Cup final

BY **MIKE GREEN**

Gloucester skipper Dave Sims receives the trophy from Nick Hale, Sales Director of Cheltenham & Gloucester.

Gloucester retained the Cheltenham & Gloucester Cup at Northampton, and not even the most biased Bedford supporter would deny they deserved to do so. It was all over from the first scrum really. Well, maybe even earlier than that. Perhaps it was really all over from the moment Samoan international Junior Paramore, later to sign for Gloucester, and Irishman Clem Boyd were ruled out by injury, condemning Bedford's lightweight pack to a mauling.

Gloucester also had a few players missing, but they had much greater strength in depth. More importantly they had England prop Phil Vickery back after injury, and his skill and know-how made it a nightmare match for the Bedford front row. Only when Vickery was in the sin bin for ten minutes in the second half were Bedford able to match Gloucester up front.

Bedford were left without much option except to run what little ball they got, but this policy cost them dear in the opening minutes. Twice they tried to find openings with long passes, twice the ball went to ground – and from an attacking position on the halfway line, they suddenly found themselves trapped in the corner having conceded a scrum near their own line. Bedford survived three pushes as the Gloucester forwards went to work, and then conceded a penalty. Gloucester opted for another scrum which produced another penalty and a final warning from referee Robin Goodliffe. Down went the scrum again, and the inevitable penalty try was awarded, with Martyn Kimber adding the conversion.

So the pattern of the game was set, for although two penalties by Tony Yapp brought Bedford back to 6-7, the Gloucester forwards knew what they had to do – and they did it well. Another scrum in the corner and – no doubt working on the principle that if they were going to concede a try, it was better to do so wide out where the conversion points might not be added – Bedford allowed themselves to be shoved backwards and No. 8 Ed

Pearce touched down. Not even this tactic worked, for Kimber converted with a great kick from the touch line. Although the Gloucester forwards continued to dominate, the next score did not come until the opening minutes of the second half. Another scrum, another push, and another try for Pearce.

Bedford's best period came while Vickery was in the sin bin. There were some sizzling runs, particularly from Joe Ewens, but for all their attacking, all they could manage was another penalty by Yapp. When Vickery returned, Gloucester resumed their domination, and a brilliant try by Sims made sure the Cheltenham & Gloucester Cup was heading back to home territory once again.

The final score was 24-9, and for Gloucester, retaining the Cheltenham & Gloucester Cup was undoubtedly the highlight of their season, their supporters racing on to the field to celebrate. For Bedford, there was the bitter disappointment of losing the final for the second year running.

GLOUCESTER
Lumsden, Johnson, Grenslade-Jones, Tombs, Beim, Kimber, Beck, Windo, Fortey, Vickery, Ward, Sims, Eustace, Carter, Pearce. Replacements: Jewell, Sanders, Harris, Stott.

BEDFORD
Howard, Whetstone, Harris, Ewens, Murdoch, Yapp, Harrison, Ozdemir, Davis, Olver, Codling, Duke, Elphick, Forster, Winters. Replacements: Hartland, Hewitt, Underwood, Elliott.

Gloucester full back Audley Lumsden evades the despairing tackle of Bedford No. 8 Roy Winters.

Safe hands.

For a range of attractive mortgages and investment accounts, backed by a track record for value and outstanding service, just get in touch with Cheltenham & Gloucester.

For more details contact us on

0800 454 305

fax 01452 373681 www.cheltglos.co.uk

Cheltenham & Gloucester

Looking after your best interests

YOUR HOME IS AT RISK IF YOU DO NOT KEEP UP REPAYMENTS ON A MORTGAGE OR OTHER LOAN SECURED ON IT

A NEW BREED: the professional rugby club

BY IAN McGEECHAN

It is three years since the game turned professional, but it is only now that the truly professional organisations are emerging – at both union and club level. To say the northern hemisphere was ill prepared is an understatement, basically, because every country saw it differently and confusion reigned. It has made officials and clubs view their position, their organisation and their development with a eye on the balance sheet and the structures required to truly reach a professional standard.

From this background emerged a new group of business entrepreneurs wanting an involvement, particularly at club level. Some wanted quick returns from their investment and gradually realised that these were not going to materialise. The second group were rugby men with successful businesses, who were prepared to be more patient but were nevertheless clear in their requirements and objective – to produce a rugby business that would break even or make a small profit in its own right. Keith Barwell at Northampton is one such owner and chairman. Northampton as a club has changed its structure and practices out of all recognition in the past three years. Without Keith Barwell, the club would not exist in its present vibrant state.

The modern rugby club has to be a powerful source of inspiration for its own local community; it also has to have world-class standards of excellence in its coaching and playing programmes. The academy at Northampton has set the standard – from junior master classes and teacher training programmes in primary schools to a full-time apprenticeship programme in which those lucky enough to be accepted work for NVQs or degrees on the one hand and have full-time mentoring and coaching with the professional squad on the other. Seventy-five per cent of the current squad are club produced; of the others, 50 per cent are world-class players.

The author in conversation with Dick Best as Northampton prepare to take on London Irish at Franklin's Gardens.

The players are also the club's front-line salesmen – by their performances they can excite and enthuse not just supporters but the next generation of rugby player. Add to that visits to schools, meetings with sponsors and media and you have the professional sports package. The players have to see themselves in this complete role.

With the professional player has come the professional support. Besides an integrated coaching staff, there has to be a full-time medical team, seven days a week where necessary. This does not mean only physiotherapists (Northampton have two full time) but also a fitness expert, dietician and doctors. Northampton have a panel of four doctors who share a rota for full-time coverage; if you consider that they also have two surgeons, one of whom is at every home game, then the depth of medical support becomes apparent. As part of the academy programme, I had plans for a full, franchised sports medicine unit based in purpose-built facilities at Franklin's Gardens. This would allow full medical support to be made available to the whole sporting community around Northampton.

In the playing season the rugby facilities at the club are in use seven days a week. This arrangement takes a heavy toll on pitches, particularly in mid-winter, and the club needs all four of its pitches in use to cope. Enter the groundsman plus two full-time staff, not to mention consultants for seed, fertilisers, irrigation and equipment. During the 12 months of the year there is one period of four weeks when the facilities are not in use. All this is a major expense, which is where the commercial support for the club comes in. The new breed of club needs a match-day capacity of between 12,000 and 15,000, with upwards of 40 corporate boxes as well as corporate entertainment areas. The requirement is to produce, on the back of a successful team, average gates of between 8,000 and 10,000. Northampton at the moment have reached 7,000 with a capacity of 10,000 – but things are already on the move!! But if there are only 15 occasions per year when the ground is full, the other part of the commercial equation is utilising the clubhouse facilities every week of the year. High-quality rooms are necessary to cater for conferences, seminars and celebratory functions, which all need a high-class environment.

Marketing is now key for the top clubs because it is this area that links facilities, sponsors, clients and players. All – not just some – of these ingredients are necessary for a club truly to be called a professional business. Even so, to make the marketplace fair, the year – that is, the season – has to be structured professionally. It is grossly unfair to turn the game professional and then not have a level playing field for the distribution of revenues. I firmly believe that the majority of revenue should go to the participants – in other words, international revenues to the unions, club/provincial revenues to clubs and provinces. Each also has to have a fair piece of the season. I must admit, I am pleased to see the Scottish districts in the Welsh League. This now gives strong domestic competitions in England, Scotland and Wales. Wouldn't it be tremendous to have the top two or four in each of these two leagues playing off for a grand British final, with the participants receiving significant prize money but all the league clubs receiving something?

The players are a club's sales force, and exciting, world-class performers like Pat Lam (here making his Northampton debut against Sale) can attract spectators to rugby matches, as well as helping to bring success.

Matt Dawson marshals his forces at Franklin's Gardens in the depths of winter. Keeping pitches in service throughout the season is an expensive pastime and a major reason why the modern professional club needs commercial support.

This sort of structure plus a European Cup would produce relevant revenue from which clubs could gain a measure of financial stability. If the competition were structured correctly, there would be high-quality competition with a high net worth. This is so important if we are to truly look after our main assets – the players. I have no time for club chairmen who insist the players need to play 52 weeks of the year because their ground facilities cater for a mere 3,000 to 4,000 spectators with few benefits – they are not professional. The new professional clubs have facilities to match the team and the team to match expectations of supporters and chairman. Pressure, yes; but an environment in which those who truly see themselves as community and business institutions will have the environment in which they can thrive.

I will never forget my last home game in charge at Northampton. Activities of all kinds in the 'Village' by the lake end of the ground – for adults and children. Various eating and drinking outlets all thriving fully two hours before kick off, and with Bath and Northampton fans mixing with good humour. Even Bath fans could have their faces painted or hair dyed! Then came a game of high quality with outstanding players on both sides. Northampton scored 40 points – Stuart Barnes and Sky were there to witness it – and 8,000-plus fans left the ground with smiles on their faces. Northampton are finally there. They have got it right. It is a family club, and everybody is welcome. The professional game is beginning to get a lot of things right; it should only get better. New breed, new rugby, new horizons.

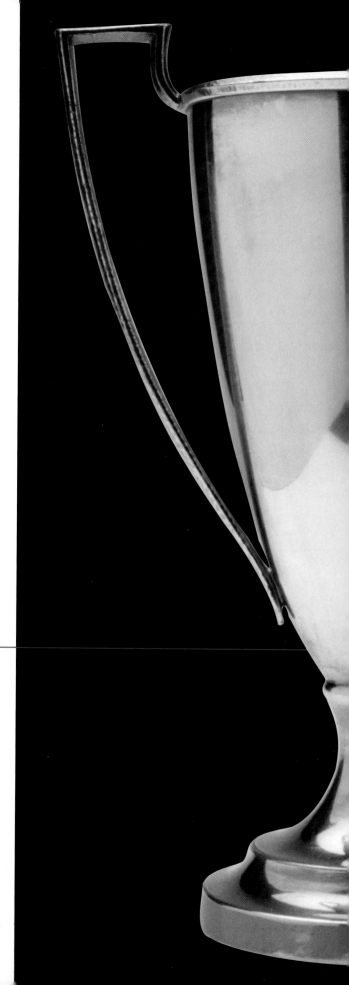

A top team in the field of law.
One step ahead of the game.

winning

Wragge&Co

55 Colmore Row Birmingham B3 2AS England

Telephone +44(0)121 233 1000 Fax +44(0)121 214 1099

e-mail: mail@wragge.com   website: www.wragge.com

THEATRE OF DREAMS

BY **EDDIE BUTLER**

No-side at Cardiff on 26 June 1999, and Wales rejoice, having beaten the world champions, South Africa, 29-19 to christen the Millennium Stadium in style.

It was always a bit of a joke, raising the governing body of a sport onto a dais from which it could survey the people and occasionally cast down droplets of wisdom. But that's what happened in Wales. For most of the 20th century, the Welsh Rugby Union enjoyed life as one of the loftier institutions in a small land.

The selectors were known as the Big Five. Doff your caps, lads. The Secretary of the WRU was an austere figure of authority. Tug your forelock, son. Because one day you might be called upon to run out at the Arms Park...

Like a Roman emperor gorging on wine and suckling pig served by castrated slaves, it was all too absurd to be true. Even before the great Welsh rugby era of the 1970s had drawn to a close, it was clear that the WRU couldn't organise a 'pissuptimus in a vineyard', as they used to say in Rome.

The committee was asked to look to the future and chose instead to put on a blindfold. Towards the end of the 1970s and at the start of the 1980s, they built a stadium – The National Ground, Cardiff Arms Park – that was out of date and too small even before it was completed. The national team was allowed to drift into decline. There were scandals over rebel tours to South Africa, sackings of Secretaries and upheavals at club level. And all that before Welsh rugby discovered it was to be contaminated by the worst disease known to man – professionalism. Wales entered the new age of the paid game with all the enthusiasm of the driver of a cart going down the main street of Merthyr shouting 'Bring out your dead'.

The national game of Wales was heading for the lime-pit. As recently as the summer of 1998, the national team suffered its worst-ever result at international level, when a shadow XV hastily assembled by yet another caretaker coach lost in Pretoria to the Springboks 13-96. And the beautiful irony was that while the game was unravelling at the speed of a committeeman's hand reaching for his allocation of free tickets, the greatest civil-engineering folly of all time was going up in the heart of Cardiff: the Millennium Stadium. Unloved, unnecessary and unbelievably costly, the stadium was to be the centrepiece of the World Cup of 1999, which meant that instead of Wales' decline remaining a sour joke for local consumption, now a mass of people from overseas could come and have a laugh, too.

And then something changed. Off came the blindfold. They were about to chuck the corpse into a mass grave when it sat up and said in a clear voice, 'Let's just check to see if Graham Henry is available'. The coach of Auckland, the Blues and New Zealand 'A' was, and nothing has been the same since. Oh, he came at a price, but when you're forking out half of £120 million for a stadium, what's another couple over five years for the best brain in the business?

Henry had days rather than weeks with his new team before their first outing at Wembley against the same Springboks who had piled on the humiliation in Pretoria. Henry's Wales nearly pulled off the surprise victory of all time, eventually going down 20-28. Wales then lost to Scotland and Ireland in the Five Nations. Were they back on the same old rollercoaster? No. From that moment Wales began a sequence of five victories on the trot, all away from home – if you count beating England at Wembley as an away triumph. France, Italy, England, and Argentina twice in Buenos Aires: a roll call of revival that says the Welsh are back.

'Let's just check to see if Graham Henry is available.' He was.

It was achieved without fuss on the part of the coach. No shrieking, no hysteria. His management team of assistants and managers – Lyn Howells, Steve Black and David Pickering – all stay calm: 'Don't get carried away. We're not there yet.' But all the while, the fragile confidence of the Welsh has been restored.

On the field, Henry has changed many things. 'We don't have forwards who can compete head on with the best,' he said when he first surveyed his options. But he has built a new front row, rejuvenating hooker Garin Jenkins, discovering Peter Rogers in South Africa and setting up an intriguing tight-head duel between the new kid, Ben Evans, and the old warrior, David Young. Henry became the first to harness the forces of the Quinnell brothers, Craig and Scott. He converted Chris Wyatt into a second row, and the former No. 8 of Llanelli instantly became the Welsh player of the year.

Behind the scrum, he picked at full back ex-All Black Shane Howarth – whose grandfather was a Cardiff docker – the first yield from the process of scouring Welsh connections in the overseas market. And then, most important of all, he stopped analysing what Neil Jenkins couldn't do and said, 'What he can do at outside half is run the game for me'. And Jenkins has done just that, playing flatter than before and continuing to kick points by the bucket-load.

And all the while, the coach kept saying, 'Hang on. We're not there yet.' But then came a sixth victory: Wales 29, South Africa 19. A home win, at the Millennium Stadium on the day the place was opened. No longer a civil-engineering folly, the Millennium Stadium, the project so dear to WRU Chairman Glanmor Griffiths, has become a theatre of dreams. It is quite simply the best rugby stadium in the world – atmospheric and intimate, yet vast in scale at the heart of the capital city. It will be the most wonderful setting for the fourth and biggest Rugby World Cup.

So, a coach and a stadium at the cutting edge of the game, a peace deal between warring clubs, a blueprint for schools of excellence, rugby reclaimed as the game of the people of Wales – all this the work of the Welsh Rugby Union. They may never be placed back on a dais from which to look down on all below, but they may have earned themselves a place at ground level, respected as a creative institution.

One of the sensations of the season – No. 8 turned second row Chris Wyatt, the Welsh Rugby Writers' Player of the Year, demonstrates his all-round skills against Ireland.

BITTERSWEET FINAL:
the Tetley's Bitter Cup

BY **NIGEL STARMER-SMITH**

The only certainty about the 1999 Tetley's Bitter Cup Final was that there would be a new name on the trophy. You could stretch a point by suggesting that there was an historical connection between Newcastle Falcons and Gosforth, the amateur club who had twice won the cup in the 1970s, but that would be the same as suggesting that there was a meaningful connection between NEC Harlequins and Harlequins FC of yesteryear. For Wasps there was a determination to assume bridal status at last and cast aside the mantle, finally, of bridesmaid. Twice in the 1980s and also in 1995 and 1998 Wasps had been runners-up. Ironically, three key players involved in one or more of those cup finals in which Wasps had appeared had subsequently formed the cornerstone of the emergent professional Newcastle club – Steve Bates, Rob Andrew and Dean Ryan.

This time, in the 28th playing of the cup final, Wasps were to make no mistake in clinching the trophy that had eluded them for so long. Without doubt Wasps entered the Twickenham arena with the decided advantage that the rest of their domestic schedule was 'done and dusted'. They had finished their Premiership league programme and had ensured that they had earned qualification as one of England's representative clubs in the European Cup. Not so, Newcastle, who had been immersed in crucial league games as recently as the Thursday prior to the final itself and still had one decisive game (versus

Saracens to be played on the Thursday following the cup) hanging over them like the sword of Damocles. That Newcastle played below par, losing both the cup final and the European-qualifying decider five days later was scarcely surprising. Nor were they helped by the absence, through injury, of the man who had for several years been their principal playmaker and performer, as well as being their Director of Rugby, Rob Andrew. Despite the undoubted precocious talents of the man who took his place, 19-year-old Jonny Wilkinson, Andrew was sorely missed.

Wasps also had the significant advantage of being able to field 12 players with cup final experience, with a resolve, no doubt, to make amends for the chastening experience meted out by Lynagh, Sella, Pienaar and co. the previous year, when Saracens had beaten them 48-18. For others, hurt and frustration had become more deeply engrained. Both Lawrence Dallaglio and Darren Molloy had played in the 1995 final (losing to Bath 16-36), while Canadian international Gareth Rees, at the time a Harrow schoolboy, had been on the losing side (again to Bath) as long ago as 1986.

In some respects it was an unremarkable game, overall; the atmosphere relatively muted in a stadium far from full, and dominated in numbers, unsurprisingly, by the close-to-home Wasps supporters. Fortunately they were able to make plenty of clamour and enjoy the celebrations, since Wasps were to rule the last threequarters of the match. Once they overhauled Wilkinson's early penalty goal they never looked back.

Perhaps the most fascinating revelation was that under the fly-half spotlight it was not Rob Andrew's protégé that shone but the Wasps' number 10, Alex King. Here was a player who a couple of seasons ago had been heralded as Andrew's natural successor in England colours. Although he had won two caps as a replacement against Argentina and South Africa while on tour, his talent had never fully blossomed. A serious knee injury had also sidelined him at a crucial time in 1998. In addition to scoring the neatest of tries with a darting clean break, as well as a fine dropped goal, it was his masterful tactical

Former Wasp Inga Tuigamala on the burst. for the Falcons. He scored his side's only try, Jonny Wilkinson adding the conversion plus four penalties.

Former Wasps Steve Bates and Rob Andrew, now calling the shots at Newcastle, look on apprehensively as their side struggle against the Londoners.

control and all-round skills that characterised the outstanding fly-half performance of the season. Wilkinson remains frontrunner for the England job, yet it would be foolish to ignore the claims of King as the man to fill the spot that has been such a problem for England since Andrew left the scene. Not yet the king but a promising heir apparent!

Elsewhere, the key battles were won by the Wasps back row, as Joe Worsley (especially), Lawrence Dallagio and Peter Scrivener excelled. Nor will Newcastle quickly forget the impact made by the pocket battleship that goes by the name of Trevor Leota of Samoa, who will be certain to cause a few dents in opposition armour when he dons the jersey for Manu Samoa in the World Cup. There was, too, the customary excellence of Gareth Rees, of the educated boots (four penalties and two conversions) and rugby brain, together with the tenacious cover defence of Josh Lewsey, who also scored a fine try that was to eclipse any lingering Newcastle hopes late in the second half. Credit, too, to Mark Weedon's leadership of a team that performed well throughout and never once looked like letting the Falcons fly.

For Newcastle, Wilkinson was unable to prosper behind a pack that lacked its normal aggression and resolution. The powerhouse up front, containing five full internationals (Graham, Nesdale, Huster, Archer and Weir), is normally an intimidating combination, and with the addition of Walton on the flank, there is wealth of experience, but on this occasion it did not fire on all cylinders. Behind the scrum there were just the occasional destructive forays of the 'Samoan All Black' – and erstwhile Wasp – Inga Tuigamala to nurture Newcastle pretensions. The cover tackle on him by Josh Lewsey was not only the champagne moment of the match but also signalled a realistic end to the Falcons' challenge. Tuigamala did once cross the line for a try but that was by way of consolation at the game's end. That score and Wilkinson's four penalties and conversion were never enough to unsettle the Wasps, who retained their movement and focus to the finish. As you'd expect of things that irritate and sting, they just kept busy. The Falcons were caged.

After the game, Rob Andrew, the Newcastle Director of Rugby, was philopsophical: 'It was hugely disappointing. There, these things happen. Wasps deserved it; their defence won them the game. There wasn't a lot in it – I wonder what might have happened if Inga had scored on his first interception and breakaway. We tried to speed things up after half-time, but we got a bit frantic. But we never exerted enough control, or steadiness on the ball to trouble Wasps. Inevitably there is a problem when there are so many late-season important matches – that is certainly one of the things that has to be sorted out. On the personal front, I'm looking ahead to a full recovery from the shoulder injury during the summer and have no intention of retiring yet.'

Inga Tuigamala, Newcastle's former All Black threequarter, was equally gracious: 'Wasps came at us with all guns blazing and minimised our attacking options. You've got to respect that; they really did play well. As for the key moment when I was caught racing for the line – well it showed I need to do a bit more speed work! We made big errors at the wrong time.'

Meanwhile, Nigel Melville, Andrew's opposite number at Wasps, had this to say: 'We had to win it – there was no point in coming to Twickenham and losing again. It's great that the club has made five cup finals; it's an immense relief to have finally capped one with a win. We said we'd be successful just as much through our defence as our attack. Newcastle seemed obsessed with throwing the ball wide and playing from very deep positions. Put a big defence up and there are few areas left for them in which to create. We left a few holes; they got through once and scored a try, but to be honest we gave them the points that they had, and ill-discipline at certain moments by us allowed them to keep it fairly close.

'We knew what to expect of Newcastle – we had played them a couple of weeks before; the only question for us was whether Tuigamala would play centre or wing – that did affect our selection but we guessed right. Gareth Rees did his usual job – he kicked the points and marshalled the defence for us from the back. The pack played well to contain the big, strong Newcastle pack and it was particularly interesting to see the two fly halves competing.

England international back Josh Lewsey runs in for Wasps' second try. Besides his attacking skills, Lewsey's defensive capabilities were in evidence at Twickenham.

'We achieved our principal ambitions for the season. What we now need is more stability and continuity next time. We've got to win more regularly and be consistently successful. In player development and financially we are going in the right direction. We are evolving as a club, but we have no player revolution or 'clear-out' each season. We sign players for two or three years and then bring younger players through behind them, who, if they are good enough, eventually take their place. So it is that the likes of Worsley, Scrivener and Lewsey have come to the fore and earned regular first-team places. Sometimes it gives us quite an advantage when late in the game the senior pro or international then comes off the bench to take over – it can have quite a significant impact on the opposition when that happens.

'Add to all this the fantastic support which Wasps are now generating. Who would have dreamed a couple of years ago that we'd be bringing so many fans and such enthusiasm to Twickenham from Loftus Road? It's going great!'

The beer flows for Wasps as they lay their hands on the cup at last. Many of their players knew what it felt like to come second at Twickenham – some had experienced it more than once! – and they weren't going to let the trophy get away again.

A VERY AMICABLE UNION
Scottish Amicable and the Barbarians

Since 1990, the Amicable Gesture – an initiative aimed
at supporting the stars of the future – has raised £108,000
for youth rugby, £300 for every Barbarian try scored

BAABAAS TAME THE TIGERS: the Scottish Amicable Trophy

BY IAN ROBERTSON

There is no doubt the fourth match in the end-of-season challenges between the English club champions and an invitation team represented a massive stride forward with the introduction of the Barbarians and Scottish Amicable for the first time. In retrospect it seems so obvious to feature the most famous club side in world rugby in this extravaganza, and for the Barbarians it is also a very welcome platform and window of opportunity. In the modern claustrophobic world of professional rugby, the Barbarians have found themselves being squeezed out of the front line of battle. The top players in England play too much rugby in the fiercely competitive world of the Premiership (26 matches last season), the European Cup (a minimum of six this season), the Tetley's Bitter Cup (an average of two or three cup ties per club) – not to mention at least seven internationals. With over 40 games as a basic diet plus four or five weeks on a summer tour there is time for just one lick of the ice cream and the new season is ready to start.

Regrettably, the glorious days of the BaaBaas Easter tour and so much of the proud history and the wonderful tradition of this great club have been consigned to the record books, and the BaaBaas have received another unwelcome dent to their heritage in recent years when teams from the southern hemisphere have not played their final tour game against them.

The fickle finger of fate has not been kind to the BaaBaas in the past three years, but happily the annual match for the Scottish Amicable Trophy should prove to be the perfect antidote. During the first three years of the series, an amorphous World XV was put together with no identity and no tradition to uphold. It was very difficult to persuade the right calibre of people to turn out and there was nothing really at stake for the players once the team had assembled. From now on all that has changed, and changed dramatically for the better. The famous players from every corner of the rugby world know the remarkable history of the BaaBaas, and they all regard it as an honour and a privilege to be selected. It was no surprise, then, to see the incredibly

Leicester flanker Lewis Moody takes on the BaaBaas. Moody scored twice for the Tigers in an 88-point feast at Headquarters.

Walter Little, who scored a first-half try, was reunited with his old All Black centre partner Frank Bunce in the Barbarians midfield.

powerful side the BaaBaas, with help from Scottish Amicable, managed to assemble at Twickenham for the last Saturday of the season. The names being floated six weeks prior to the match all sounded very high powered and very exciting. To the surprise of the cynics and the delight of rugby supporters they all turned up to produce a really outstanding side.

The major Unions all have the highest respect for the BaaBaas and everything they stand for, so they showed genuine willingness to release their players. Most important and significant of all, the players wanted to come and play for the Barbarians. How else do you explain a famous All Black like Glen Osborne flying 13,000 miles from New Zealand just to sit on the replacements' bench? The BaaBaas produced a side bristling with exciting talent. To start with they had one of the best attacking full backs in the game in Springbok André Joubert. Outside their brilliant half backs, Thomas Castaignède and Agustin Pichot, they had arguably the best international centre partnership of the 1990s in All Blacks Frank Bunce and Walter Little.

And just imagine the captain of Italy, flank forward Massimo Giovanelli, answering the phone to be told by the indomitable and much-revered President of the Barbarians, Micky Steele-Bodger, that he had been selected for the BaaBaas to play alongside the two most celebrated back-row players of the last ten years – All Black Zinzan Brooke and Springbok World Cup winning captain François Pienaar. Dreams do not normally come this good.

To coach this multi-talented group of stars, the Barbarians invited the 1991 World Cup winning coach, Australian Bob Dwyer. The BaaBaas don't do things by half. It was gratifying, then, that the crowd of 40,000 was more than double the previous year's total, and this augurs really well for the future. The weather was kind and the two teams put on a first-class game of rugby.

Although Leicester lost four league matches out of 26 they were quite clearly the best team in the Premiership, and it is a tribute to the Barbarians that in a most competitive but highly entertaining match they outplayed and outscored Leicester by nine tries to five. In the process they recorded the highest score and the biggest victory in the series. The margin of the win was certainly no disgrace to Leicester because they were facing a superb, world-class team, and to their credit they played their part to the full in making this a memorable match and a great occasion.

The BaaBaas were always in control and after racing to a lead of 21-7 with tries from André Joubert, Walter Little and Zinzan Brooke they finished up 31-14 ahead at half-time. Even though Leicester scored two tries before half-time and another three in the second half they spent the last 40 minutes never better than 12 points adrift. With Glen

Osborne scoring two tries in the second half and South African James Small and French wing Philippe Bernat-Salles one each the Barbarians topped the 50 points and became the first winners of the Scottish Amicable Trophy. If in the years ahead they can continue to pick BaaBaas sides of this calibre it could be a while before an English club prises the trophy away from them.

BARBARIANS
André Joubert, Philippe Bernat-Salles, Walter Little, Frank Bunce, James Small, Thomas Castaignède, Agustin Pichot, Os du Randt, Raphael Ibanez, Martin Scelzo, Abdelatif Benazzi, John Langford, Massimo Giovanelli, Zinzan Brooke, François Pienaar. Replacements: David Hilton, Marco Caputo, Doddie Weir, Wayne Fyvie, Joost van der Westhuizen, Lisandro Arbizu, Glen Osborne.

LEICESTER
Geordan Murphy, David Lougheed, Craig Joiner, Jon Stuart, Austin Healey, Pat Howard, Jamie Hamilton, Derek Jelley, Richard Cockerill, Darren Garforth, (Captain) Martin Johnson, Fritz van Heerden, Lewis Moody, Martin Corry, Paul Gustard. Replacements: James Ferris, Tim Stimpson, Mark Meenan, Graham Rowntree, Dorian West, Adam Balding, Neil Back.

Scorers
BARBARIANS Tries: Joubert (2), Little, Brooke, Castaignède, Small, Osborne (2), Bernat-Salles. Conversions: Castaignède 5.
LEICESTER Tries: Ferris, Moody (2), West, Rowntree. Conversions: Murphy 4.

The victorious BaaBaas, complete with coach Bob Dwyer and Micky Steele-Bodger, reflect on a fine afternoon's work, having beaten the Tigers 55-33. The participation of the Barbarians can only enhance the reputation of this end-of-term fixture.

THE PLAYERS' VOICE: the PRA

BY DAMIAN HOPLEY

Against a background of power struggles and financial mismanagement in rugby, the Professional Rugby Players Association (PRA) was launched in August 1998, three years to the day after the game had gone 'open'. The past 12 months has seen a dramatic turn around in the fortunes of professional Rugby Union in this country. From the disasters of record defeats in the Antipodes to the formation of an amalgamated 'super club', it is safe to say that these days nothing comes as a surprise in rugby any more.

After much consultation with the leading players in the game, it became clear that the one voice missing throughout the teething problems of professionalism was that of the players. While many current professionals gave up good careers to concentrate on full-time rugby, and receive some handsome salaries in to the bargain, few were prepared for the possible pitfalls that lay ahead. The response from the players has been overwhelming, with over 400 players joining the PRA in our first year, paying a subscription of £100.

Our primary purpose in the PRA, therefore, is to provide much needed welfare for the players. Every single member receives legal insurance to cater for any contractual disputes and disciplinary action. One only has to look at the infamous Kevin Yates scenario to see the extreme issues that can arise. Our expert panel of solicitors is spread out across the country, so we are in a position to provide our players with much-needed legal advice as required.

We have also improved the disability insurance that every player in the Premiership has to protect them against career-threatening injuries. Statistics show that the intensity of the game has increased fivefold in the past couple of years. Only last season some 20 players or so retired from professional rugby due to injury, the most notable being the Welsh captain, Gwyn Jones. The current generation of players are all very privileged to earn handsome salaries from doing something they love, but the shelf life of any sportsman can be extremely short, so there is a overwhelming need for players to look after themselves.

Given that the game is still in its professional infancy, the prevalent attitude tends to be that 'It won't happen to me'. So when a player is forced to retire from the game prematurely it is unfortunately too late to help. Having been in the unenviable position of having to leave the game early, the feeling of what might have been lingers on.

The next area that we have been concentrating on is the commercial representation of the players. That is not to say that we act as an agent for individuals, but we are in the process of establishing a code of conduct for agents, in an effort to stamp out some of the cowboys who may see young rugby players as an opportunity to cash in.

The launch of the PRA 'In Touch' Business Partnership is providing the association with much-needed revenue in its first few years. Through the partnership there will be access to first-class players and the quality events that the PRA runs over the year.

Our third objective is the provision of career and education training for our members. Be it through work placements, full-time or part-time education, there is an onus on the players to prepare themselves for life after their playing careers. Rugby is tremendously fortunate in that many of the players at all levels have had the basis of a very good education. Our concern, however, is that the career span of any professional player is getting increasingly shorter, so the players should be using their considerable 'down time' to good effect, with one eye on the 'after-life'.

Many traditionalists have shied away from professionalism, citing that the sport has sold its soul and by doing so has lost many of the characteristics that have made it the sport that we all enjoy so much, both on and off the pitch. However, it is always going to prove a difficult marriage between that emotion and the hard-headed nature of business as we come to terms with the fact that our sport is now a multi-million-pound industry. There is no perfect solution. People will always have problems with professionalism, and the constant political machinations that have dominated the newspaper headlines have not helped anyone involved in the sport. However, I am increasingly confident that with a viable structure in place the sport has a very bright future indeed.

Simon Fenn and Kevin Yates pack down against one another ten months on from the infamous ear-biting incident. That episode was an extreme example of why the PRA provides legal insurance to its members.

The 1999 Rugby World Cup in the British Isles provides a wonderful opportunity to celebrate all that is great about the game. With 20 competing countries playing across the realms of the Five Nations, it will be a heady mixture of playing styles and cultures, and the interest in the game will reach unparalleled heights. The climax of the tournament at the Millennium Stadium will be a fitting way to reflect on a century of rugby in a country that has thrilled so many fans over that time (for example, 11 April 1999!).

To David Roberts and all our friends at Wooden Spoon Society, we welcome your continued support and this opportunity to spread the word in this yearbook. It has been a lively start for us in our first year at the PRA, and given the overwhelming endorsement we have had from our players, we are looking forward to next season and many more to follow. To date, we are still seeking funding from the RFU and the leading clubs, but recent indications are that they will both be supporting the PRA and its objectives. We look forward to working alongside both bodies to further the cause of the game and its key assets – the players – into the Millennium and beyond.

For further information about the PRA, please contact the offices:
Tel: 0171 580 3979 Fax: 0171 580 3989

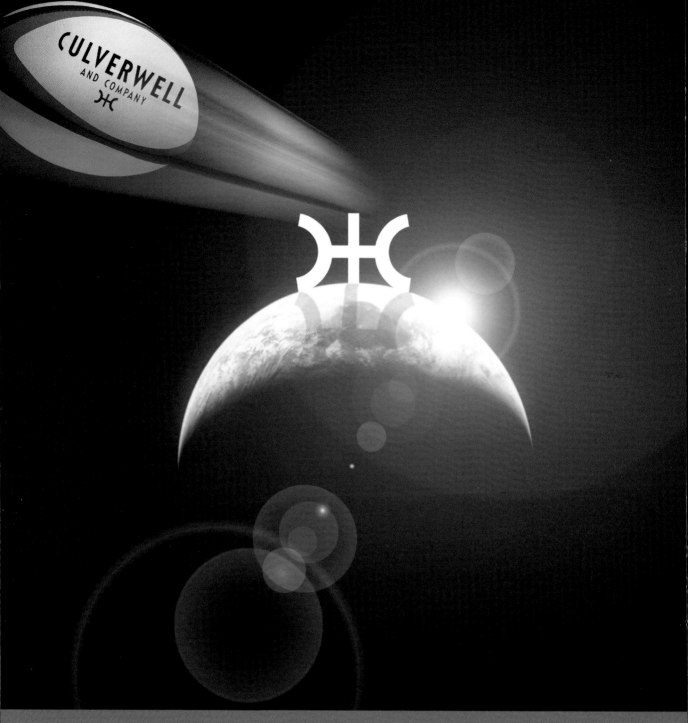

REVIEW OF THE
SEASON 1998-99

REACH FOR THE BEST

It's rare to find a recruitment consultancy who tackle personnel requirements with such tenacity and unfailing dedication. An unrivalled approach that has enabled Pertemps to remain unchallenged at the top of the league as the UK's leading independent recruitment consultancy.

As market leaders, we have developed our reputation not just by "filling positions" but by adding value to our client portfolio, a philosophy which is reflected in the diverse range of leading blue-chip companies that currently utilise our services.

Operating in three service divisions: commercial and professional, industrial and driving and technical and executive, our fully integrated service ensures that we are able to deliver quality personnel with the right skills, in the right place at the right time.

So, if you are seeking to win the competition for business, make sure that you retain the competition for talent by choosing Pertemps, Britain's most successful independent recruitment consultancy.

PERTEMPS
recruitment partnership
....

Head Office: Meriden Hall, Main Road,
Meriden, Warwickshire CV7 7PT.
Tel: 01676 525000 Fax: 01676 525009

THE LLOYDS TSB FIVE NATIONS CHAMPIONSHIP

BY **BILL McLAREN**

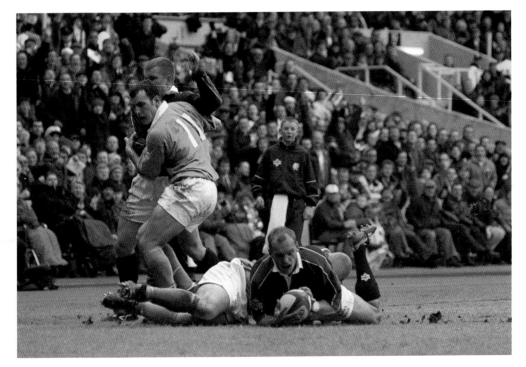

Gregor Townsend touches down during Scotland's 30-13 victory over Ireland at Murrayfield. In this final Five Nations Championship, Townsend joined the select band that have scored tries in each leg of the campaign.

Seldom in the history of the Five Nations Championship has there been a more riveting or more dramatic climax than there was to the 1999 event, when England had the Grand Slam dashed from their grasp at the final hurdle so that Scotland, with a little help from Wales, became the last Five Nations champions (Italy join for season 1999–2000). Scotland took the title for the first time since their Grand Slam of 1990, and they took it on points differential.

It was an extraordinary Five Nations which not only spawned some glittering interplay and 45 tries but also underlined the lows and highs of Welsh participation, showed up Irish promise that was not quite realised, and included the unexpected victories in Paris by Wales and Scotland that left the might of France at the bottom of the final championship table. In particular there were those closing two days – 10 and 11 April – on which two totally unforeseen results in Paris and at Wembley brought despair to England, unfettered joy to Scotland and delight for Wales in having beaten the two acknowledged heavyweights, France and England, in quite dramatic style.

Imagine the scenario! Scotland so excelled themselves in Paris as to draw from their Director of Rugby and coach, Jim Telfer, the view that he never had seen them play as well. Despite the funereal version of 'Flower of Scotland' by the local band they endured prior to kick-off, then despite conceding a try in two minutes by Christophe Dominici,

Neil Jenkins feeds Gareth Thomas as Wales progress towards a dramatic win over England at Wembley. Jenkins contributed eight goals from eight attempts in the match, but he proved beyond doubt in this championship that there is more to him than his right boot.

Scotland put together some pacy passages with adventurism written all over them. With full back Glenn Metcalfe demonstrating the counterattack and intrusion brilliance of his previous season with Glasgow Hawks, Alan Tait choosing astute running linkage lines, and Gregor Townsend silencing his critics with a display of balance, judgement and restored skill levels, Scotland won by five tries to three, by 36-22. In a quite extraordinary first half, 53 points were registered, and when Townsend sizzled in narrow confines for his try he joined that distinguished quartet, each of whom has scored a try in each match of the Five Nations Championship – Carston Catcheside (England, 1924), Johnny Wallace (Scotland, 1925), Patrick Estève (France, 1983) and Philippe Sella (France, 1986). However, having lost to England by 24-21 at Twickenham on 20 February in a match in which England were quite awesome for the first 20 minutes but which Scotland could have won had Kenny Logan not missed three kickable penalty goals, the Scots knew that they could win the championship only if Wales beat England.

The 1999 championship also delivered two of the most entertaining matches ever seen. When Wales beat France 34-33 in the Stade de France on 6 March, seven tries were scored. There was an avalanche of 46 points in the first half, with Emile Ntamack, the French full back, scoring three times and Neil Jenkins startling the whole of France by lying flat and crossing the gain line at pace as well as kicking seven goals. His worth to his country can be measured in his 64 points out of Wales' 109 in the campaign, a record by a Welshman in a championship.

No scriptwriter could have concocted a more nerve-tingling tale than naturally evolved from the pulsating action of the Wales v England match at Wembley on the sabbath, 11 April. England were ahead in two minutes from a cracking try by Dan Luger after a loop between Mike Catt and Matt Perry. The English loose forwards, Richard Hill, Lawrence Dallaglio and Neil Back, with augmentation from Tim Rodber, kept the door closed with quality defending to which former Rugby League coach Phil Larder had contributed so much during squad sessions. Yet Neil Jenkins, with six penalty goals and his conversion of Shane Howarth's try, kept Wales in contention at 25-31, at which point England opted for a penalty touch at the corner instead of seeking safety points with a penalty goal attempt going into injury time. Whereupon Chris Wyatt underlined his magnificent line-out contribution, with ball creamed off the top Scott Quinnell thundered towards midfield before releasing Scott Gibbs, who came onto the ball like a super-charged motorboat to leave four defenders adrift. Of course the winning conversion still had to be slotted, but the man most would have chosen to take on such a high-pressure task, Neil Jenkins, put it plumb to a roar of approval from thousands of

England's Jonny Wilkinson slots one of his five goals against Ireland. Wilkinson's goal-kicking, distribution and bone-crunching tackling marked him out as one of the backs ot the championship.

his countrymen that could have been heard in the Rhondda Valley! 32-31: Neil Jenkins eight goals out of eight attempts, and Scots everywhere raising their glasses to their own championship heroes – and to Wales!

It had to be a curious campaign by Wales following their wonderfully spirited performance in going down 20-28 to the world champions, South Africa, in November. Wales had lost to Scotland by 33-20 at Murrayfield on 6 February, the championship having been launched in dramatic fashion by a crafty Scottish ploy. To start the game, Scotland stand-off Duncan Hodge switched his kick to the left as a tester for the new Welsh wing Matthew Robinson. At the dropping point, Scotland's New Zealand centre, John Leslie, 6ft 2ins and rising like a rocketing pheasant, ripped the ball clear prior to charging 40 metres for a sensational try that took only ten seconds in the scoring, the fastest try ever recorded in an international. It was an indication of how Scotland hoped to perform in the championship that against Wales they won the rucks/mauls by 71-30 and crossed the gain line 73 times to 46 by Wales. The Man of the Match award went to Scotland lock Scott Murray (Bedford), who formed with Stuart Grimes a new and effective engine room in the injury absence of Doddie Weir.

In beating Ireland at Murrayfield by 30-13, Scotland excelled in gaining turnover

ball. This match saw the Melrose hooker, Steve Brotherstone, gain his first cap as a replacement after 15 games on the bench and there was also what was then described as 'the try of the century'. This score had Scottish self-belief written all over it as Gregor Townsend from the deep, Glenn Metcalfe, Alan Tait and Cameron Murray all handled before that elongated lock Stuart Grimes gave an impressive demonstration of intuitive support running to put the finishing touch.

Scotland deserved their championship. They put together some thoroughly exciting interplay for a rich haul of 16 tries; their midfield of Townsend, Tait and John Leslie was a potent force, with Townsend's play blossoming in the creative presence of Leslie and the astute choice of running angles by Tait. The Scots also had the nucleus of a pack that will serve them for some years – Tom Smith, Gordon Bulloch, Scot Murray and Stuart Grimes with Eric Peters in great form at No. 8, plus the massive Blue Bull tight-head Matthew Proudfoot in the wings after a frustrating injury absence.

England's pack had some memorable passages and deserved a better scoring return from their backs considering the quality of ball that they churned out like chocolate bars from a slot machine. England out-muscled Ireland and gave them no space as Kyran Bracken's decision-making proved highly impressive. Also England produced one of the backs of the

Above: A dejected and dye-stained Jeremy Davidson trudges off after last-gasp defeat against France.
Right: One of the few high spots of a dismal campaign for France was Christophe Dominici's early try against Scotland.

Scotland coach Jim Telfer and his players congratulate each other after winning the final Five Nations Championship with a magical performance in Paris. It was Telfer's last Five/Six Nations match in charge.

championship in Jonny Wilkinson, who, still just 19, kicked five goals and delivered a gem of a floated pass for Matt Perry's try in the 27-15 defeat of Ireland, then slotted a record-equalling seven penalty goals in the 21-10 defeat of France, in which prop Jason Leonard gained his seventieth cap. England might have beaten Wales had they potted that penalty goal instead of seeking touch at the corner.

The Irish flattered to deceive. They hinted at high potential in holding France to 10-9 in Dublin on 6 February, but David Humphreys landed only three of seven penalty-goal attempts and Thomas Castaignède gave France victory with a late penalty success. This was the match in which players became covered in the blue and red dye of the sponsors' logos.

The Irish then enhanced their record over Wales, to whom they hadn't lost since 1983, with victory at Wembley by 29-23, Humphreys this time being the hero with 19 points, including two crucial dropped goals and a charge-down of a Jenkins punt for the try by Kevin Maggs. Some powerful running by flanker Dion O'Cuinneagain marked the Irish performance at Murrayfield, while England had conceded 22 offence kicks against them in Dublin. The Irish pack proved a match for any, but Ireland were short of creativity and penetration in midfield, which was mirrored in their meagre haul of just three tries from four championship games.

For France this season was a disaster. They had a new flying machine in Dominici, but their midfield was defensively vulnerable. They conceded to Wales a first win in Paris since 1975, they should have been put to the sword by England, and they were unable to cope with Neil Jenkins' aggressive running or with Scotland's brilliance in taking on a French style against the French.

So Scotland became outright Five Nations champions for the fourteenth time, deservedly so when one examines the tries scored and conceded table as well as the final championship places.

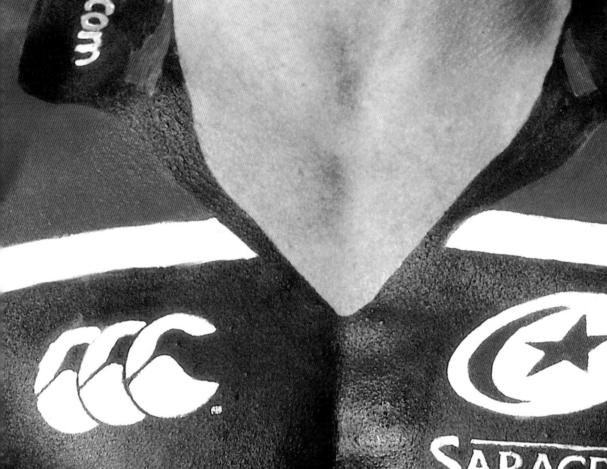

THE CLUB SCENE

ENGLAND – Trouble and strife

BY BILL MITCHELL

To say anything other than that this was a disastrous season for English rugby would be to be economical with the truth. All the strife, the domestic problems, the bankruptcies – everything – were self-inflicted, and there is nothing available to suggest that there is any real light at the end of the tunnel. Never before has English rugby been held in lower public esteem – the English situation is worse than those in Scotland and Wales, where there are also troubles.

The 1998–99 season started off on the wrong foot with the EFDR (English First Division Rugby) clubs failing to issue a fixture list until a few days before the campaign was scheduled to start. This was due to the fact that Cardiff and Swansea were in dispute with the WRU and had refused to take part in their domestic league programme but, apparently against the wishes of the RFU in Twickenham, had been offered a full fixture list by EFDR, a list that was mostly fulfilled, with Allied Dunbar's ultimate champions, Leicester, taking top place in the unofficial table narrowly from Cardiff. It was greatly to the credit of the competition sponsors, Allied Dunbar, that they made no public condemnation of the clubs' procrastinating behaviour.

It had always been all too obvious that the top clubs followed the decrees of their 'sugar daddy' bosses, whose interests were purely commercial. The same clubs, for reasons that were hardly logical, also refused to take part in any form of European competition, which was undoubtedly a contributory factor towards the financial problems that most of them almost immediately had to face, with the ultimate tragedy of the demise of both Richmond and London Scottish.

The former could be attributed to an astonishing decision by Richmond's management to move their operations to a new and not properly completed stadium in Reading, where they had some good crowds but none big enough to cover their weekly costs, which had been inflated by the presence of an expensive playing staff. Their 'Mr Money', Ashley Levett, had justified his move by claiming that Richmond were 'dead in the water' at the Athletic Ground, but it did not take long after his decision for the drowning process to be completed.

Meanwhile, Richmond's co-tenants London Scottish moved expensively to the Stoop Memorial Ground and fired their administrative staff to cut costs. Their sugar daddy, Tony Tiarks, soon joined negotiations with Bristol (who were seeking insurance against a possible failure to

Wasps scrum half Andy Gomarsall gets the undivided attention of Swansea's Andy Moore in the clubs' Anglo-Welsh clash in September 1998.

regain their top division status) to sell the club and thus destroy it. The process of execution was eventually effected but not through any sale to the West Country. Instead, the two erstwhile co-tenants merged with London Irish.

Further bad publicity came the way of English rugby when the country's most successful ever captain, Will Carling, revealed in an autobiography that he intended to end his association with his partner Ali Cockaigne, the mother of his son. Carling had managed to evade any punishment for his off-the-cuff 'old farts' comments a few years earlier, but there was to be no escape for him this time and a planned testimonial match for him at Wembley Stadium on 5 December 1998 had to be abandoned when it became clear that the public no longer had any enthusiasm for the idea. The excuse that this was a private matter could not be invoked, since it was through the author's choice no longer private – and the reputation of the game suffered further.

The ultimate crisis came at the end of the season, when EFDR decided that only a dozen clubs were needed in the top division. Richmond provided a form of legal – if not moral – justification for their effective expulsion from the top flight through every fault of their own, as they had been taken over by receivers; all their professional staff were thrown out of their jobs with the consequent loss of much-needed personal incomes. This episode plus the antics of Mr Tiarks at London Scottish meant that the two 'fall guys' required had been found, although not without much protest from the victims.

If all that was not enough, the RFU came into conflict with the other Five Nations countries over television revenues to the extent that England's future in the competition was in jeopardy, and England's charismatic captain, Lawrence Dallaglio, was accused of personal malpractices by the *News of the World*, but that matter is still effectively *sub judice*, so one can happily say nothing about it.

Amid all the behind-the-scenes mayhem it must be said that some excellent rugby was played with probably the highest standard of skills ever seen in England. The numerous foreign players along with several home performers did produce some exceptional matches, and with six clubs qualifying for the European competitions in the new season, all the Premiership top division sides had something to play for right up to the end of the campaign. At the finish Leicester were worthy champions by a comfortable margin of six points over Midlands neighbours Northampton, with Saracens, Harlequins, Wasps and Bath, who have struggled in the last two campaigns, joining them in Europe. London Irish narrowly 'missed the cut' after on many occasions looking one of the most enterprising clubs in the whole competition, although they tended to belie their name by fielding few players with Irish international qualifications; it will be interesting to see the playing composition of the new merged club next season.

Bedford's Charlie Harrison is caught by Dean Ryan of Newcastle Falcons. Bedford finished second-bottom of Premiership One but survived the drop by beating Rotherham in a close-run two-legged play-off.

At the foot of the table West Hartlepool played gallantly but were out of their depth, while Bedford, who finished one place above them, survived a two-legged play-off against the luckless Rotherham by scoring an extra try over the two games after an aggregate tie (38-38). The Yorkshire club, which has come a long way since the leagues were originally started, had again been thwarted cruelly at the play-off stage of the campaign.

In the Premiership second division there was an exciting competition, with Bristol ultimately coming out on top ahead of Rotherham after the ambitious Worcester club had looked like foiling them both for much of the season. Injuries and a lack of adequate cover in all positions were Worcester's ultimate downfall, but they are determined to succeed and have the backing to do so.

It was sad to see Blackheath and Fylde propping up this table, and their places have been taken by Henley, another very ambitious outfit, and Manchester from the top Jewson National League, whose two regional second divisions were led by Preston Grasshoppers (North) and Bracknell (South). The fact that such previously underrated clubs are now in a position to challenge the best – finances permitting – says much for the league system, which will also see such welcome fresh names joining the senior ranks in the new campaign as Doncaster, Bedford Athletic, Westcombe Park (from Orpington in Kent) and Penzance & Newlyn, who have a great and romantic history; many will hope that they will now bring fresh honours to the far reaches of the country.

Luke Nabaro of Premiership Two champions Bristol is tackled by former Leicester Tiger John Liley, now of Worcester who finished in third place in the division.

Billericay of Essex beat Silhillians from Birmingham 19-3 to lift the Tetley's Bitter Vase.

The Tetley's Bitter Cup provided good consolation for the top players, who had missed out on Europe, but surprise results in the early rounds were few and far between. The fourth round did provide a shock as former finalists and joint winners Moseley lost at home to Lydney (24-25); in the following round the highly fancied Northampton team lost badly at home to London Irish.

The quarter-finals then produced two close games, with Harlequins (at Gloucester) and Leicester (against Richmond in Reading) both losing 15-13, but holders Saracens were well beaten at Newcastle, and London Irish could not cope with incessant Wasps pressure at Loftus Road (19-3) before a club record crowd of 11,417.

Richmond by now were looking down at financial doom and had no real chance when faced by Newcastle in Reading (20-3), but Wasps had a tougher home task against Gloucester (35-21) before advancing to their fifth final. Gloucester's consolation was that they again won the Cheltenham & Gloucester Cup by repeating their 1998 final victory over Bedford (24-9).

The Twickenham final finally brought a cup success for Wasps, who won more comfortably than the ultimate 29-19 scoreline suggested. Newcastle's Jonny Wilkinson for once had an indifferent game and in contrast Wasps, well led by Mark Weedon and including such star names as Josh Lewsey, Rob Henderson, Kenny Logan (after half-time), Alex King and Lawrence Dallaglio, never appeared to be threatened.

In the earlier finals there were Twickenham victories in the NPI Trophy for Aldwinians from Manchester (21-10 against Midlanders Dudley Kingswinford) and in the Tetley's Bitter Vase for Billericay from Essex (19-3 victors over Silhillians from Birmingham's approaches). The finals may have been low-key affairs in the end, but long may the two competitions continue, providing as they do an opportunity for a day out for loyal junior club supporters.

The County Championship still has a loyal following, particularly in the West Country – so it was perhaps appropriate that Cornwall and Gloucestershire should contest the final. The descendants of Trelawny, who had avenged their Twickenham defeat by Cheshire in the 1998 final by winning their semi-final at Redruth (35-16), came out on top in a rousing match with a 24-15 victory over Gloucestershire, who had themselves reached the final by eliminating Lancashire 23-20 in extra time at Vale of Lune. Yorkshire's Under 21s prevented a Cornish double by thrashing their Under 21s 41-15 in the curtain-raising final.

The Middlesex Sevens were won by an invitation Penguins side, which shaded a thrilling final against Saracens (40-35). The Army (not surprisingly when their greater resources are considered) retained the Services crown, although the Royal Navy gave them a worthy battle in their showpiece match at Twickenham.

The Varsity match again attracted a near-capacity attendance. Cambridge won for a fifth successive time, although the final 16-12 score did not really reflect their superiority on the day. Oxford's lock Russell had to cry off on the eve of the game, and the Dark Blues did themselves no favours by rearranging their pack to meet the emergency, with the result that their fine No. 8, Challender, was made to play at lock; his effectiveness was diminished accordingly.

The BUSA title went to Swansea, who thrashed St Mary's College (Twickenham) 35-15, while the now sadly devalued Hospitals Cup saw the conglomerate Imperial Medicals win a tight encounter with Guy's (21-12).

There was still plenty to amuse and entertain fans, but the successes of the season were achieved in spite of and not because of good organisation from the top, and the RFU administrators have numerous problems on their plates. Have they the will to face them and re-establish their control of the game as they must if in England at least it is not to be brought into further disrepute? The soul of the game is in desperate danger of being destroyed. Is anyone prepared to stand up and fight to his last breath to defend it?

Cambridge's boiler-room partnership, the brothers Hamish and Angus Innes, home in on the Bowring Bowl after the Light Blues prevailed once again in the Varsity Match.

BEHIND SCOTTISH RUGBY.

SCOTLAND – Heriot's this time

BY BILL McLAREN

Heriot's FP celebrate in style after winning the SRU Tennents Scottish Premiership Division One title. They last won the Scottish title in 1979, when they were led by Andy Irvine.

They made a declaration of intent by coming out of their blocks like starving greyhounds for 119 points in their first three performances against Glasgow Hawks, Jed-Forest and Watsonians, and they came to the wire in equally devastating fashion with 164 points from their last three games. In between they didn't do badly either!

Heriot's FP were popular Scottish Premiership Division One champions in 1998-99 because they imparted a much-needed breath of fresh air to the Scottish club scene shorn of its top competitors. The club, of course, has spawned eight Scottish international full backs, among them that prince of adventurous entertainers, Andy Irvine. He was the last player to have captained Heriot's FP to the Scottish title. That was in 1979.

In claiming the 1999 Division One championship Heriot's FP embraced a style that, in a sense, had Irvine written all over it – a thoroughly attractive, fluent method that had them putting most opponents to the sword and that, in the crucial last match of the campaign against the 1995 champions, Stirling County, rattled in ten tries to four in an away victory by 75-25. Their championship win was an achievement all the more remarkable in that Heriot's FP in the previous season had escaped relegation by a whisker through winning a tense, late decider against Kelso. Thus Heriot's FP underlined

Former Melrose back Rowen Shepherd in action for the Glasgow Caledonians Super District side. Did the formation of Super Districts devalue the Scottish Premiership by siphoning off too many of the best players? Some people thought so.

their status as always having been in the top division of the Scottish National Leagues and Premiership since the start in 1973-74. The former Scotland hooker Ken Milne, Heriot's FP Director of Coaching, explained that they had been working for two years on 'getting the ball out wide' and that had now paid off. 'We want to get back to the old values of club rugby at Heriot's. We want sides at every level in the club to be playing attractive rugby,' he said.

There were those who undervalued the Heriot's 1999 feat as having been achieved in the absence of quality performers withdrawn from club sides to fuel the efforts of the Super Districts – Glasgow Caledonians and Edinburgh Reivers. Certainly Watsonians, Melrose and the previous season's Division Two champions, Glasgow Hawks, in particular, had lost a number of class men in this fashion. However, Heriot's FP themselves had lost a number of quality players in the previous season and entered the 1998-99 series with a very young, inexperienced outfit, notably in their back division, which contained right wing Charlie Keenan (21) and stand-off Gordon Ross (21) of the 1995 Scottish Schools side, and Ross, full back Gregor Lawson (20) and Stewart Walker (21) of the 1996 Scottish Schools squad that had toured South Africa. The pack also contained the 19-year-old loose forward Simon Taylor, Scotland's Young Player of the Year, and the 21-year-old Andrew Dall, whose brother, Graham, a tourist with Scotland in Zimbabwe in 1995, formed with Taylor and the 23-year-old Tammas McVie perhaps the most formidable loose-forward trio in the championship.

Such faith in youth was amply justified, for in the 18 games of the Premiership, Heriot's registered 75 tries, of which 52 were by their daring young backs. Walker proved a lethal finisher, with a rich haul of 17 tries, some as the result of interplay with his Dollar Academy schoolmate, Gregor Lawson – son of Alan, the former Scotland scrum half – whose sizzling augmentation of attack ploys proved a thrilling and productive ingredient. Simon Taylor topped the forward try scorers with eight, and Keenan's six tries, which owed much to startling acceleration, included three in the closing Premiership game with Stirling County. Their stand-off, Ross, was top scorer in Division One with 351 points that included 285 in the Premiership. It was hardly surprising that he was presented by Graham Fraser with the President's Prize at the club's annual dinner.

Heriot's FP allied set-piece efficiency to pack mobility, their slimline lock Andrew Dall playing a full and influential role in line-out provision and in handling linkage. Heriot's had talented runners in their pack, and their speedy recycling at the breakdown point enabled their exciting young backs to stitch together some delightful passages, with Walker, Keenan and Lawson excelling as finishers.

Such long-awaited success afforded immense pleasure and satisfaction to their 36-year-old captain and loose-head prop, John Bryce, a rock-hard builder, who led from the front, was forthright in play and speech, and kept stoking the fires of the Heriot's FP forward play with his rumbustious charges and dogged scrummaging. Bryce had been with

Heriot's FP for 14 years and this was his first major success with them. The Heriot's style also owed much to their coaches – former Ebbw Vale flanker Gareth Davies and Donald McDonald – and to their team manager and Director of Rugby, Fraser Dall, for encouraging their young players to trust their instincts in seeking an attractive pattern of play. Perhaps the one disappointment for Heriot's FP was their inability to beat Melrose, champions in 1990, 1992, 1993, 1994, 1996 and 1997 and strong favourites to regain the title. Having lost at home to Melrose 23-30, Heriot's opted in the return game in January to play against the wind, were 0-17 down at the break and lost 3-22.

Melrose, of course, still were renowned as a drive and post pack, with the veteran Robbie Brown as an inspirational figure to the younger element represented by Millan Browne, Craig Smith, James Henderson and the 19-year-old hooker Wayne Mitchell. As always, Melrose gave opponents minimal time on the ball and sometimes none at all. They had genuine pace behind from Mark Moncrieff, Chris Dalgleish, Steve Laurie and Bruce Ruthven, a clever playmaker in internationalist Scott Nichol, and a new orchestrator in the former Gloucester stand-off Alex Morris. Melrose suffered the heaviest of their four defeats at the hands of a youthful West of Scotland side by 24-0, Melrose appearing jaded and missing the likes of Craig Chalmers and Carl Hogg. West eventually just avoided the drop and yet carried some impressive young potential in the likes of lock Craig Hamilton, New Zealand full back Guy Curtis and the flying machine that is Rory Kerr.

Where Melrose felt they had 'blown' their championship chances was in the 27-25 defeat away to Hawick on 23 January. In mud and rain Hawick adapted more sensibly to the conditions, suggesting that their developing young side might be quite a handful in the next season, not least their right wing Neil Douglas, who scored three tries against Melrose – and that happens very seldom!

Melrose lock Scott Aitkin rises to the occasion during his side's 22-3 defeat of Heriot's. The Greenyards club completed a league double over the eventual champions.

Currie weren't quite consistent enough although formidable when all the cogs were meshing. Yet they had the distinction of beating Melrose twice, partly because Currie's big pack matched their rivals and because Currie had one of the great match winners in Scotland 'A' stand off Ally Donaldson, who in the second game against Melrose on 12 December scored all Currie's points in a victory by 19-18.

Coached by Bruce McNaughton, Currie were in the title race until the closing stages, for they had beaten Heriot's FP by three penalty goals to one on 30 January, but late defeats by Glasgow Hawks and by Boroughmuir, coached by former Scotland centre Sean Lineen and former Scotland No. 8 Iain Paxton, placed them in fourth position.

Despite losing the services of Derek Stark, Glenn Metcalfe and playmaker Tommy Hayes, Glasgow Hawks did exceptionally well under the captaincy of David Wilson to finish in third place, considering in the previous season they had been in Division Two. They had a gifted addition to the squad in stand-off Eugene Martin, who had played for New Zealand Youth and Maoris. He called the shots with Cameron Little, his partner in wake of a pack that contained Gavin Walsh, a New Zealand prop, Andrew Plastow, a large No. 8 from Brisbane in Australia, and a prolific line-out source in Charles Afuakwah, a 32-year-old dental surgeon in Greenock.

Following their opening 31-13 defeat by Heriot's FP, the Hawks ran up eight wins and a draw from their next nine games, but defeats by Hawick, Boroughmuir and Melrose

The victorious Gala team parade the SRU Tennents Velvet Cup through the streets of Galashiels after their 8-3 Murrayfield victory over Kelso.

ruined their title hopes, although they did gain the second-highest number of match points – 54 to Heriot's 56. Hawks' trouble was that they could raise only seven bonus points whereas Heriot's FP's more flamboyant style fetched 13.

Sadly for Boroughmuir, who had been outright National League champions in 1991, they were relegated to Division Two for next season, along with Stirling County, champions in 1995. It was a particular blow to Boroughmuir, who always had been in the top division, and equally so to Stirling, who had failed to win any of their 18 games, their one draw (21-21) being against Jed-Forest at Riverside Park.

Meanwhile, Gala and Kelso gained promotion back to Division One. Gala were not only Division Two champions but also winners of the Scottish Cup, with an 8-3 win over Kelso in the final at Murrayfield, and winners of the prestigious Melrose Sevens tournament, with victories in semi-final and final over, respectively, the powerful South African sides Stellenbosch University and Villager. It has been quite a season for the Braw Lads of Gala, and it means that among the ten teams in Division One next season there will be five clubs from the Border country – Melrose, Hawick, Jed-Forest, Gala and Kelso. That should make the city dwellers sit up, take notice, and look to their laurels!

WALES – An unsatisfactory year

BY DAVID STEWART

The quick summary: a messy, disjointed and unsatisfactory year. Prices up, crowds down, the challenge of igniting and sustaining the public interest is still to be met. Welsh folk still like their rugby football; enough made the trek to Wembley three times to prove that. The danger for the game's domestic future is the one already facing Scotland and Ireland – plenty of fringe followers come to the big attractive international fixtures but find alternative pursuits on other weekends between September and April, leaving a small bedrock of committed fans.

Cardiff and Swansea, the Principality's two biggest and (in theory) strongest professional clubs spent the summer of 1998 wrangling with the Welsh Rugby Union, cosying up to the English senior clubs for inclusion in the Allied Dunbar League, only to be excluded by the gentlemen at Twickenham representing the (English) RFU. A series of 'friendlies' against the English first division clubs followed. An enlightened ten-year-old could have predicted what followed – some entertaining, high-intensity early-season fixtures, but by the time league points started to really matter for the English clubs and international calls came, second-string outfits were fielded. The two Welsh rebels kept on winning of course, merely inflating their self-measurement of quality and ability. Cardiff were brought crashing back to reality when Llanelli humiliated them in a SWALEC Cup semi-final in one of the few games that really mattered to their opposition.

Swansea fly half Arwel Thomas looks for support as he is caught by Llanelli's Mike Voyle in the SWALEC Cup final. Swansea eventually prevailed 37-10.

Above: Swansea's
Tyrone Maullin takes on
the London Irish backs.
Below: Former Wales
and British Lions scrum
half Terry Holmes
parted company with
Cardiff in 1998-99.

The rebels' absence meant the (again) unsponsored league was less competitive and accordingly less well supported. Modest crowds saw some bold and entertaining rugby, but with power and skill some way short of what is on offer elsewhere in Europe – as results in the Heineken Cup painfully bore out. Swansea were probably the best side last term. Their reluctant leader, Scott Gibbs, inevitably led from the front, and shrewd (aren't they all?) Kiwi John Plumtree got the best out of a squad that contained the ideal blend of old soldiers (Paul Moriarty), established internationals (Garin Jenkins, Colin Charvis, Mark Taylor), and classy youngsters (Ben Evans and Darren Morris). They crushed Llanelli 37-10 in the SWALEC Cup final – played for the first (and one assumes, only) time at Ninian Park. One whimsical observation: the ground capacity increased for a rugby match; you see, we don't have to segregate supporters, unlike soccer crowds (and long may that continue). A secret of the All-Whites continuing success will be their engine room, containing Andy Moore (too skilful to be out of international rugby for long if he stays injury free) and Natal import Tyrone Maullin (with a name like that – and being one of the less dubious southern hemisphere imports – surely the selectors of one of the home nations must be able to unearth something interesting on the genetically manipulated – GM – family tree front). Young James Griffiths will increasingly challenge these two.

Llanelli took the other main item of silverware, the Premier Division title. It was not their fault that it was a devalued competition with the rebels elsewhere. Yet again they were coached by Gareth Jenkins, the best home-grown coach (and one of the nicest men) in Welsh rugby, who is now assisted by retiring centre Nigel Davies. The Scarlets showed their quality in beating league runners-up Pontypridd no less than five times. The

disappointment of failing to do the 'double' will ease in their memory when they recall the Brewery Field 39-10 destruction of old rivals Cardiff in April in the penultimate round of the cup (which sparked a major changing of the guard for the losers). Stability returned to Stradey. The ground was developed under the ownership of the WRU, and once again it will play host to a World Cup match. With Llanelli's landlords also financing team-building, Scott Quinnell and John Davies were high-profile and high-impact returnees from exile in Richmond. Watch for the developing talent of fly half/inside centre Stephen Jones. Again, an effective boilerhouse combination was crucial – spring-heeled international team-mates Mike Voyle and Chris Wyatt (the Welsh Rugby Writers' Player of the Year), with the developing Vernon Cooper in support.

Pontypridd and Cardiff are close geographically but not at all emotionally. Ponty, the most consistent club of recent years, experienced an unhappy close-season. Lyn Howells, assistant to Graham Henry, was not on contract and was thus gratefully snapped up by the Arms Park club when they parted company with Terry Holmes. There was the on/off saga of Neil Jenkins' transfer, and flanker Martyn Williams also followed the coach on the short journey down the A470 to the capital. A number of the city 'rejects' were offered to Ponty, but the only one of real interest was Lee Jarvis, a fly half they groomed themselves before he became yet another who failed to flower in the blue and black. Ponty's playing season was mixed. Some sublime rugby was on display at times, such as the March mauling of a young Bridgend side by 73-14, with capped players Dafydd James and Geraint Lewis well to the fore. By contrast, a limp home display in October saw unheralded Treviso triumph by 22-13 and dent an honourable record in Europe to date, one which alas will become increasingly difficult to sustain. Loss of key players is part of the problem. Off the field, in the battle to be the fourth WRU superclub (after Cardiff, Swansea and Llanelli), the Sardis Road club can point to a track record of achievement. Newport, however, in a professional game can provide a growing commercial hinterland and a wider (not to say more affluent) spectator base. Those who

Pontypridd wing Dafydd James in action during Wales' Five Nations victory over England at Wembley in April 1999. Ponty are bidding to become the fourth Welsh superclub after Cardiff, Swansea and Llanelli, but they had an up-and-down season in 1998-99.

delight in skilful running-and-handling back play will hope Kevin Morgan and Gareth Wyatt will be provided with sufficient ball by a pack of forwards that needs reinforcing on grounds of both age and firepower.

Cardiff have some fine established players, some improving ones, like prop Spencer John, and a few exciting young 'uns, such as Rhys Williams (full back), Jamie Robinson (centre) and Phil Wheeler (wing forward). They also have some rather ordinary and overpaid ones who need to find an extra gear if the club is to prosper under the leadership of the three H's – Howells, Humphreys and Howley. They can do it, and Graham Henry in particular wants to see them fly the flag for Wales in the European Cup.

The nursery of talent that is the Gnoll had a more satisfying time than the previous season. The WRU had bailed Neath out of financial administration. Rugby-wise, former international wing forward Lynn Jones was a thoughtful and creative coach who contributed in provocative fashion to the public debate about the Union's plans for a superclub system and the inclusion of the rebels directly into the European Cup. Third place in the league saw Neath pip Ebbw Vale for a place in that lucrative competition. They are likely to find the level of play on the other side of Offa's Dyke every bit as difficult as they did in 1998–99.

Ebbw Vale lost a key league match (to Neath) by a missed penalty; credibility, when undergoing a 106-18 hammering at Toulouse in November; players in Kingsley Jones and Byron Hayward; and another Euro-Cup spot, when their fourth place did not count following the WRU/rebels peace deal. They gained an interesting new coach in former Bath and Gloucester man Richard Hill. Caerphilly had the best of the newer top-flight coaches in Chris Davey, the former Maesteg hooker; the most consistent points scorer in Brett Davey (apart from the mighty Jenks, naturally); one of the best results – 31-20 against Racing Club in Paris in October; and a highly creditable fifth place.

Bridgend had their usual season. They played some eye-catching stuff, brought on some promising younger players, like back-rower Gavin Thomas and hooker Gareth Thomas, and are probably resigned – no WRU money or superclub status for the fertile rugby soil of mid-Glamorgan – to losing many of them as usual, à la Devereux, Hall, Howley, James, Gareth Thomas (the threequarter version) et al. Their highlight was an unexpected 20-15 home win over the recently mighty Brive in November. The best things about Newport were their cerebral coach, Allan Lewis, and their young centre Matthew Watkins, who remarkably was the only player who appeared throughout every league game. His form as much as his fitness saw him rewarded with an Argentinian trip with the national side. Aberavon went down (again) to be replaced by promoted Dunvant (again), who may find life at the top no easier than last time around.

Just maybe, the future is a little brighter. The marvellous win over the Springboks sent the rugby folk of the nation into summer with renewed expectation for the game in Wales. A winning national team in a stadium that all can be proud of may be just the tonic to reinvigorate the club scene. The agreement between clubs and Union, albeit one born out of economic necessity, provides a structure and clarity sadly missing in 1998–99. But when the choice boils down to Leicester v Saracens on satellite TV, the DIY store, playing with the kids, or Neath v Dunvant/Ebbw Vale v Bridgend, will the paying punter opt for the local fare? It is a long and perhaps unlikely road back to the days of a decade and more ago when large crowds flocked to all the best first-class fixtures. The professional era may well have to exist on modest spectator numbers and concentrate increasingly, like soccer, on developing other income streams.

Oh, one other thing – thank you very much, Mr Henry!

IRELAND – Ulster victorious

BY SEAN DIFFLEY

The highlight of the Irish season was the European Cup victory of Ulster over Colomiers in that memorable final at Lansdowne Road on 30 January. The ground was packed, 30,000 of the 50,000 travelling down from Ulster. The enthusiasm was terrific, and, indeed, the feat of Ulster, coming through against Edinburgh Reivers, Toulouse in the quarter-final, Stade Français in a frantic semi-final at Ravenhill, and then that final victory over Colomiers, ranks as one of the finest achievements in Irish rugby. It's not many sides that can boast of beating three top-rated French clubs in succession.

It all reflected great credit on their modest coach Harry Williams and on a very committed squad of players. Two of those were particularly effective – the outside half, that skilled footballer David Humphreys; and the remarkably consistent place-kicker, full back Simon Mason. It was a 21-6 final win, and it all demonstrated that there is true and attractive competition in Europe. The return of the English clubs should add immensely to that competition.

There were some good performances by the other provinces as well, with Munster getting to the quarter-finals; they went down to Colomiers, having already beaten

Ulster full back and goal-kicker Simon Mason, who landed six penalties out of six attempts in the European Cup final.

Perpignan, Neath and Padova. Leinster beat Bègles-Bordeaux and Llanelli but were beaten by Stade Français, and Connacht, in the European Shield, could not live up to their previous season's performances, losing three of their six ties.

It has not all occurred by accident, of course. The structures put in place by the IRFU are beginning to work after the initial teething troubles caused by both the arrival of the professional game and the loss to the Irish game – in the first season of professionalism – of leading players going abroad. Irish rugby because of its relatively small number of players could ill afford such draining of resources. After all, the Irish game has a total of 201 clubs and 242 schools. England's RFU, as an example, has 1,958 clubs and 3,072 schools affiliated.

Those new structures negotiated by the IRFU with the four provinces has resulted now in contracts for 61 full-time and 41 part-time players representing their respective provinces. However, it's not just that senior players like Eric Miller and the Irish captain, Dion O' Cuinneagain, are playing in Irish domestic rugby: the promising youngsters are being persuaded that the far-off hills are not as green as they were led to believe. Good packages put in place by the Union are convincing them that there is a brighter future at home.

In the All-Ireland League the emphasis is still very much on the very committed Munster clubs. The only difference this past season is that the emphasis shifted slightly – from Limerick to Cork. This season's winners were Cork Constitution, with Shannon, the Limerick club that had won the competition for the previous four seasons, fading to sixth place and out of reckoning, losing five of their 11 ties. The format in the first division was the same as it was in the previous season (in which it was introduced for the first time), with the 12 teams playing 11 ties and the top four then taking part in semi-finals and a final. It was a controversial idea when first introduced, but it has worked out well on both occasions.

The top four were Garryowen and Cork Constitution from Munster, Buccaneers from Connacht and St. Mary's College from Leinster. The real surprise packets were Buccaneers. Comparatively new, they are an amalgamation of the old Athlone and Ballinasloe clubs, and they produced some stirring moments and attracted an enthusiastic following as they pursued their merry way. However, Constitution, coached by former

Irish scrum half Michael Bradley, were just that bit too experienced for Buccaneers and beat them 32-20. The other semi-final, played in Limerick, saw St. Mary's College lead 17-0 at half-time, only to succumb to a powerful second-half resurgence by a determined Garryowen, who went on to win the match 19-17 in typical Limerick style.

The final at Lansdowne Road was a hard-fought affair. The teams were locked together 11-11 at full-time, but the Cork side took the trophy with a winning penalty kick in the first period of overtime. The IRFU president, a noted Constitution stalwart, Noel Murphy, had the pleasure of presenting the trophy to the winners.

For next season it has been decided that a system of match and bonus points will be introduced. Bonus points have been part of the format in the Guinness Inter-Provincial championship, and obviously the scheme has been considered a success. The idea is that four points will be awarded for a win, two for a draw, one point for scoring four or more tries, one bonus point if beaten by seven points or less. If nothing else it will ensure that observers will not be nodding off.

There will be further changes the following season, 2000–01, when the four divisions of the All-Ireland League will be changed into three divisions of 16 clubs, each division being divided into two sections of equal merit, with clubs playing each other home and away. The top two in each section will then qualify for semi-finals in which the winner of one section will play the runner-up of the other. This applies to all three divisions, with finals at Lansdowne Road.

Overall, Irish rugby is in a healthy state, both from a playing and from a financial point of view. At schools, youths, colleges, Under 21, and 'A' levels, and despite the relatively meagre rugby population, the game flourishes. The concern, of course, is to have the national side returning to more winning ways. But there is confidence that under the team management of Donal Lenihan and the coaching of Warren Gatland such will be achieved.

It's a costly business. Last season the player and coaching costs amounted to just over £6 million, an increase on the previous year of almost £1½ million. But the Union, as it has for most of the century, remains 'in the black'. But they do admit that 'in this professional time we are stretched to meet our commitments'. And they are conscious, too, that the question of upgrading Lansdowne Road or seeking a new stadium looms in the future. All decisions have been postponed pending the result of a government feasibility study on the question of a suggested national stadium. Nobody is holding their breath on that one.

The Irish are confident that Warren Gatland and Donal Lenihan can improve the fortunes of Ireland's national side.

FRANCE – Number 15 for Toulouse

BY CHRIS THAU

Their first title was in 1912; their fifteenth, out of 20 appearances in the French Championship final, was in 1999, when they defeated in a grim and perhaps unappealing battle the formidable challenge of Montferrand. In between there was a century of 'red and black' passion and romance.

An inspired scribe observed that while two of the legendary clubs of French rugby, Béziers and Lourdes, have had the label 'Great' attached, in order to identify a certain period in their otherwise undistinguished history, Toulouse have never been called the 'Great Toulouse'. This is simply because, even through the leanest period in its history – for 31 years, between 1948 and 1979, Toulouse failed to reach a championship final – there has never been any doubt about the greatness of the club.

Didier Lacroix, Xavier Garbajosa and Emile Ntamack parade the French Championship trophy after Toulouse's victory over Montferrand.

However, the aftermath of the 100th championship final was marred by controversy, with Montferrand's international flanker Arnaud Coste accusing Toulouse of underhand tactics and singling out his fellow international, prop Franck Tournaire, as the villain of the piece. Toulouse captain Franck Belot was cool and unrepentant: 'I am surprised by his comments. There is no doubt that the best has won. I always respect my opponents and it is sad that Montferrand are not showing the respect we deserve.'

Other than that, the new professional league has proved a great success, with attendance up 20 per cent from the previous season. Serge Blanco, the new president of the Professional League, has settled in nicely after a few tussles with both the FFR and the more militant of his directors. France secured themselves a nice cut out of the European Cup and Shield, while Grenoble, under Michel Ringeval, managed to recapture their giant-killer status after a fairly poor patch.

While for Toulouse it was business as usual, the former champions Stade Français had to wait until the final of the Cup to secure themselves a place in Europe next season. Diego Dominguez and his cosmopolitan colleagues, who include in their ranks the gifted Richard Poole-Jones – already forgotten by England selectors – beat Bourgoin 27-19 to secure the last major trophy of the season. For a substantial number of Stade Français regulars, this was their last season under the Parisian sun, as they prepare to return to their roots in the Southwest – Blond, Simon, Viars, Dourthe, Moscato, Gimbet to name just a few.

After nearly four decades in the wilderness, Mont de Marsan, one of the great clubs of the French Southwest, have made a spectacular comeback. Featuring Fijian wizard Waisale Serevi, the club of the Boniface brothers won the second division title – what the French call *Elite 2* – which will enable the team of Patrick Nadal to return to *la crème de la crème* of French rugby. Immediately the local club has offered the Fijian, who injected life and pace in the local back division, a new two-year contract, with the added incentive of playing alongside the outstanding scrum half Stephane Castaignède, recruited from Montferrand.

Elsewhere in the various leagues of the French Championship, Aubenas beat Graulhet 25-24 and Limoges prevailed 20-10 over Lyon University in *Nationale 1* and *B* respectively; the ladies from Caen beat Herm 25-12 in the final of the women's *Première* division with Villeneuve d'Ascq securing promotion from the second, thanks to their narrow 22-20 win over Bordeaux. The students from Annecy University won the student league, while in the Counties Challenge, Armagnac Bigorre beat Périgord Agenais 28-20.

Returning to Stade Toulousain, the Rolls-Royce of French rugby, one must understand that the club's success story is in its very fabric. It is the pride and indeed the achievement of becoming a playing member of a remarkable rugby entity; it is the allegiance to a club philosophy that is sound and proper. This combination of factors, from history and tradition to culture and allegiance, has given the club an almost legendary status. Toulouse is the Manchester United of rugby.

Toulouse's free-running French international prop Christian Califano is held fast this time by the Montferrand defence.

Similar to the English soccer giant, the element that has set Toulouse apart is continuity. The current coaches, Guy Noves and Daniel Santamas, have served the club as players and as junior and mini coaches. Before them, Jean-Claude Skrela and Pierre Villepreux played and coached the club to one of the most successful decades in its history.

The Bouclier de Brennus was not the only trophy acquired by the Toulouse club this year, and here resides the secret: the club has acquired two further national titles, both at junior level – *Crabos* and *Cadet A* – something as important, argues club President René Bouscatel, as winning the French Championship for the fifteenth time. 'Ideally, the "zero signing" option is what I hope to achieve within the club. In other words, I want the club self-sufficient in talented players with the stars of the future filtering through from within the ranks. I do not want to sign new players all the time. I would rather use players we bring up ourselves. This is our philosophy of development and good housekeeping.'

A SUMMARY OF THE SEASON 1998-99

BY **BILL MITCHELL**

INTERNATIONAL RUGBY

SOUTH AFRICA IN BRITISH ISLES
NOVEMBER & DECEMBER 1998

Opponents	Results
Glasgow Caledonians	W 62-9
WALES	W 28-20
Edinburgh Reivers	W 35-10
SCOTLAND	W 32-10
Combined Irish Provs	W 32-5
IRELAND	W 27-13
Ireland 'A'	W 50-19
ENGLAND	L 7-13

Played 8 Won 7 Lost 1

ARGENTINA IN EUROPE
NOVEMBER & DECEMBER 1998

Opponents	Results
Italy 'A'	W 31-9
ITALY	L 19-23
French Barbarians	L 30-38
FRANCE	L 14-34
Wales 'A'	W 28-19
WALES	L 30-45

Played 6 Won 2 Lost 4

FIJI IN EUROPE
NOVEMBER & DECEMBER 1998

Opponents	Results
Penzance & Newlyn	W 53-5
Oxford University	W 46-8
Cambridge University	W 49-13
Bristol	W 58-28
Glasgow Caledonians	L 22-41
Edinburgh Reivers	W 30-27
Leeds	L 10-27
Leicester	W 22-16

Played 8 Won 6 Lost 2

NEW ZEALAND MAORIS IN SCOTLAND
NOVEMBER 1998

Opponents	Results
Edinburgh Reivers	W 69-3
SCOTLAND XV	W 24-8
Glasgow Caledonians	W 53-15

Played 3 Won 3

AUSTRALIA IN EUROPE
NOVEMBER & DECEMBER 1998

Opponents	Results
France 'A'	W 24-9
FRANCE	W 33-21
ENGLAND	W 12-11

Played 3 Won 3

AUSTRALIAN SCHOOLS IN CANADA & BRITISH ISLES
DECEMBER 1998 & JANUARY 1999

Opponents	Results
Canada 'B'	W 35-3
CANADA	W 63-13
Munster	W 24-7
Leinster	W 13-10
IRISH SCHOOLS	W 22-12
SCOTLAND YOUTH	W 54-10
Scotland 'A'	W 41-9
England North	W 21-12
England South	W 15-10
Wales Schools Chairman's XV	W 64-3
WALES SCHOOLS	W 56-10
England 'A'	W 9-3
ENGLAND	W 21-9

Played 13 Won 13

IRELAND IN AUSTRALIA
MAY & JUNE 1999

Opponents	Results
New South Wales Country	W 43-6
New South Wales	L 24-39
AUSTRALIA	L 10-46
AUSTRALIA	L 26-32

Played 4 Won 1 Lost 3

WALES IN ARGENTINA
MAY & JUNE 1999

Opponents	Results
Buenos Aires XV	L 29-31
Tucuman	W 69-44
ARGENTINA	W 36-26
Argentina 'A'	L 34-47
ARGENTINA	W 23-16

Played 5 Won 3 Lost 2

ENGLAND IN AUSTRALIA
JUNE 1999

Opponents	*Results*
Queensland	W 39-14
AUSTRALIA	L 15-22

Played 2 Won 1 Lost 1

SCOTLAND IN SOUTH AFRICA
JUNE & JULY 1999

Opponents	*Results*
Border	W 31-28
Northern Free State	W 38-24
Mpumalanga	L 15-28
Golden Lions	L 31-33

Played 4 Won 2 Lost 2

ITALY IN SOUTH AFRICA
JUNE 1999

Opponents	*Results*
South West Districts	L 10-43
SOUTH AFRICA	L 3-74
Boland	L 17-45
SOUTH AFRICA	L 0-101

Played 4 Won 0 Lost 4

FRANCE IN SOUTHERN HEMISPHERE
JUNE 1999

Opponents	*Results*
WESTERN SAMOA	W 39-22
TONGA	L 16-20
New Zealand 'A'	L 24-45
NEW ZEALAND	L 7-54

Played 4, Won 1, Lost 3

LLOYDS TSB FIVE NATIONS
CHAMPIONSHIP 1999

Results

Ireland	9	France	10
Scotland	33	Wales	20
England	24	Scotland	21
Wales	23	Ireland	29
France	33	Wales	34
Ireland	15	England	27
England	21	France	10
France	22	Scotland	36
Wales	32	England	31

	P	W	L	F	A	Tries	Pts
Scotland	4	3	1	120	79	16	6
England	4	3	1	103	78	8	6
Wales	4	2	2	109	126	9	4
Ireland	4	1	3	66	90	3	2
France	4	1	3	75	100	9	2

OTHER INTERNATIONAL
MATCHES 1998-99

RUGBY WORLD CUP QUALIFYING MATCHES
(Held in the British Isles)

Pool 'A' (Dublin)

Ireland	70	Georgia	0
Georgia	23	Romania	27
Ireland	53	Romania	35

	P	W	L	F	A	Pts
Ireland	2	2	0	123	35	4
Romania	2	1	1	62	76	2
Georgia	2	0	2	23	97	0

Pool 'B' (Huddersfield)

England	110	Netherlands	0
Italy	67	Netherlands	7
England	23	Italy	15

	P	W	L	F	A	Pts
England	2	2	0	133	15	4
Italy	2	1	1	82	30	2
N'lands	2	0	2	7	177	0

Pool 'C' (Murrayfield)

Scotland	85	Portugal	11
Spain	21	Portugal	17
Scotland	85	Spain	3

	P	W	L	F	A	Pts
Scotland	2	2	0	170	14	4
Spain	2	1	1	24	102	2
Portugal	2	0	2	28	106	0

PACIFIC RIM CHAMPIONSHIP (EPSON CUP)

Japan	23	Canada	21
Japan	44	Tonga	17
USA	30	Tonga	10
Canada	29	Fiji	40
USA	25	Fiji	14
Japan	37	Western Samoa	34
Canada	13	Western Samoa	17
Western Samoa	6	Tonga	6
Fiji	16	Japan	9
USA	31	Japan	47
Canada	17	USA	18
Western Samoa	27	USA	20
Tonga	37	Fiji	39
Tonga	18	Canada	10
Fiji	15	Western Samoa	27

	P	W	D	L	F	A	Pts
Japan	5	4	0	1	160	119	19
Western Samoa	5	3	1	1	111	91	17
USA	5	3	0	2	124	115	14
Fiji	5	3	0	2	124	127	14
Tonga	5	1	1	3	88	129	7
Canada	5	0	0	5	90	116	4

ASIAN CHAMPIONSHIPS

Final

Japan	47	Hong Kong	7

Third-place Play-off

Thailand	38	Malaysia	8

DO YOU KNOW YOUR RUGBY?

With a Sporting Index spread bet you can BACK your opinion against ours before a game starts <u>and</u> after the off. So, if you have views on how a Rugby match will turn out then you should open an account with Sporting Index, the market leaders in sports spread betting.

CHOOSE FROM THE WIDE VARIETY OF BETS WE OFFER:

SUPREMACY
The winning points margin between the favourite and the underdog.

TOTAL POINTS
The total points scored in a game (by both sides!)

TEAM PERFORMANCE INDEX
The team gains points for winning, each try and successful goal kicks. It loses points for missed goal kicks, bookings and dismissals!

TIME OF 1st TRY
The minute the 1st try is scored (if at all!)

TIME OF 1st SCORE
The minute the 1st point is registered.

AND MANY MORE . . .

Every live TV game is traded 'In-Running' so it will never be a dull match. Every point scored (or not scored!) might mean money to you.

☎ **0171 840 40 40** FOR A **FREE INTRODUCTORY** GUIDE TO SPREAD BETTING

See our latest prices on C4 Teletext P.604 & Sky Sports Text P.361
In-Vision Sky Sports Text P.381

PLEASE SEND ME A SPORTING INDEX INTRODUCTORY GUIDE TO SPREAD BETTING — WS

NAME:

TITLE   INITIALS   SURNAME

ADDRESS:

POSTCODE:

PHONE: FAX:

SPORTING INDEX
The No.1 in Sports Spread Betting

OTHER

Italy	23	France XV	49
Scotland	30	Italy	12
Italy	21	Wales	60
Ireland	39	Italy	30
France	62	Romania	8
N Zealand	71	Western Samoa	13
Wales	29	South Africa	19

'A' INTERNATIONAL RESULTS

FIVE NATIONS

Ireland	26	France	25
Scotland	8	Wales	20
Wales	40	Ireland	29
England	27	Scotland	16
France	17	Wales	20
Ireland	21	England	28
England	24	France	21
Scotland	31	Ireland	21
France	23	Scotland	16
Wales	32	England	25

	P	W	L	F	A	Pts
Wales	4	4	0	112	79	8
England	4	3	1	104	90	6
France	4	1	3	86	86	2
Scotland	4	1	3	71	91	2
Ireland	4	1	3	97	124	2

OTHER 'A' MATCHES

Scotland	61	Italy	6
Italy	24	Wales	23
Ireland	73	Italy	14

UNDER 21 INTERNATIONAL RESULTS

FIVE NATIONS

Ireland	24	France	9
Scotland	20	Wales	22
England	38	Scotland	13
Wales	24	Ireland	18
France	6	Wales	10
Ireland	21	England	5
England	26	France	30
Scotland	13	Ireland	22
France	27	Scotland	14
Wales	36	England	21

	P	W	L	F	A	Pts
Wales	4	4	0	92	65	8
Ireland	4	3	1	87	51	6
France	4	2	2	72	74	4
England	4	1	3	90	102	2
Scotland	4	0	4	60	109	0

OTHER UNDER 21 MATCHES

England 'A'	19	South Africa	33
England	32	South Africa	10
Scotland	54	Italy	0
Italy	19	Wales	78
Ireland	54	Italy	14

YOUTH INTERNATIONAL RESULTS

FIRA YOUTH CHAMPIONSHIPS
(HELD IN WALES)

Quarter-finals

Wales	29	Argentina	5
France	25	South Africa	33
Ireland	24	Italy	15
New Zealand	74	Canada	0

Semi-finals

Ireland	15	New Zealand	21
Wales	10	South Africa	10

(Wales won on penalties count-back)

Final

Wales	0	New Zealand	25

HOME NATIONS

England	6	Scotland	21
Wales	15	Ireland	10
Ireland	19	Scotland	5
England	9	Wales	17
England	15	Ireland	12
Scotland	11	Wales	16

	P	W	L	F	A	Pts
Wales	3	3	0	48	30	6
Ireland	3	1	2	41	35	2
Scotland	3	1	2	37	41	2
England	3	1	2	30	50	2

OTHER

Scotland	15	Italy	10
Romania	25	Wales	19
Italy	5	Wales	13
England	10	France	10

SCHOOLS 18 GROUP MATCHES

France	52	Scotland	15
Italy	5	Wales	13
France	30	Wales	20
Ireland	8	England	6
England	10	France	29
Scotland	8	England	29
Wales	0	Ireland	41
Wales	9	England	16

STUDENTS INTERNATIONALS

Scotland Univ	18	Wales Univ	40
England Univ	42	Scotland Univ	20
Wales Univ	28	Ireland Univ	8
Ireland Univ	8	England Univ	40
England Students	18	France Students	18
Wales Students	19	England Students	17

THE TIMES INTERNATIONAL UNIVERSITIES TROPHY

Quarter-finals

Brunel (Eng)	18	UC Dublin	16
Grenoble (Fra)	27	Loughborough (Eng)	10
UC Cork (Ire)	23	Northumbria (Eng)	13
Trinity Carmarthen (Wal)	10	Harper Adams (Eng)	17

Semi-finals

Brunel	0	Grenoble	17
UC Cork	64	Harper Adams	7

Final

Grenoble	10	UC Cork	14

HONG KONG SEVENS

Cup Final

Fiji	21	New Zealand	12

Plate Final

Japan	33	Scotland	31

Bowl Final

Hong Kong	24	Uruguay	12

OTHER MAJOR SEVENS FINALS

Emirates:

Fiji	31	New Zealand	22

Japan:

New Zealand	12	Fiji	7

Dubai:

France	40	Natal	7

Paris:

Australia	38	England	14

Commonwealth Games:

New Zealand	21	Fiji	12

TRI-NATIONS CHAMPIONSHIP 1999

Australia	32	South Africa	6
New Zealand	28	South Africa	0
New Zealand	34	Australia	15
South Africa	18	New Zealand	34
South Africa	10	Australia	9

Final game – Australia v New Zealand – still to be played at the time of going to press.

WOMEN'S FIVE NATIONS CHAMPIONSHIP 1998-99

Results

Ireland	0	France	24
Scotland	23	Wales	0
Wales	26	Ireland	0
England	34	Scotland	7
France	34	Wales	5
Ireland	0	England	56
England	13	France	8
Scotland	22	Ireland	3
Wales	11	England	83
France	46	Scotland	18

	P	W	L	F	A	Pts
England	4	4	0	186	26	8
France	4	3	1	112	36	6
Scotland	4	2	2	70	83	4
Wales	4	1	3	42	140	2
Ireland	4	0	4	3	128	0

FIRA WOMEN'S EUROPEAN CHAMPIONSHIP 1999

Semi-finals

England	0	France	19
Scotland	9	Spain	11

Final

France	13	Spain	5

Third-place Play-off

Scotland	15	England	13

CLUB, COUNTY AND DIVISIONAL RUGBY

ENGLAND

Tetley's Bitter Cup
Quarter-finals

Gloucester	15	Harlequins	13
Newcastle	15	Saracens	0
Richmond	15	Leicester	13
Wasps	19	London Irish	3

Semi-finals

Richmond	3	Newcastle	20
Wasps	35	Gloucester	21

Final

Wasps	29	Newcastle	19

Tetley's Bitter Vase Final

Billericay	19	Silhillians	3

NPI Pensions Cup Final

Aldwinians	21	Dudley Kingswinford	10

Allied Dunbar Premiership
Premier One

	P	W	D	L	F	A	Pts
Leicester	26	22	0	4	771	423	44†
Northampton	26	19	0	7	754	556	38†
Saracens	26	16	1	9	748	583	33†
Harlequins	26	16	1	9	690	653	33†
Wasps	26	15	1	10	717	506	31†
Bath	26	15	0	11	698	574	30†
London Irish	26	15	0	11	703	607	30
Newcastle	26	14	0	12	719	639	28
Richmond	26	10	2	14	720	715	22*
Sale	26	9	1	16	604	731	19
Gloucester	26	9	1	16	554	643	19
London Scottish	26	8	0	18	491	734	16
Bedford	26	6	0	20	541	840	12
West Hartlepool	26	3	1	22	501	1107	7

Relegated: West Hartlepool

Premier Two

	P	W	D	L	F	A	Pts
Bristol	26	22	0	4	848	418	44
Rotherham	26	22	0	4	756	336	44
Worcester	26	18	0	8	716	409	34*
London Welsh	26	17	0	9	662	552	34
Leeds	26	16	0	10	713	387	32
Exeter	26	14	1	11	591	598	29
Coventry	26	14	0	12	652	560	28
Orrell	26	12	0	14	566	483	24
Waterloo	26	12	0	14	419	634	24
Moseley	26	10	0	16	498	633	20
Rugby	26	9	0	17	425	660	18
Wakefield	26	6	0	20	469	812	12
Blackheath	26	5	0	21	419	842	10
Fylde	26	4	1	21	375	805	9

Promoted: Bristol
Relegated: Blackheath and Fylde
† denotes Europe qualifier
* denotes points deducted

Jewson National Leagues
1st Division champions: Henley
Runners-up: Manchester
2nd Division North champions:
         Preston Grasshoppers
Runners-up: Stourbridge
2nd Division South champions: Bracknell
Runners-up: Esher

Tetley's Bitter County Championship
Semi-finals

Cornwall	35	Cheshire	16
Lancashire	20	Gloucestershire	23

(after extra-time)

Final

Cornwall	24	Gloucestershire	15

Tetley's Bitter U21 County Championship
Final

Yorkshire	41	Cornwall	15

University Match

Oxford U	12	Cambridge U	16

University Second Teams Match

Cambridge U	20	Oxford U	38

University U21 Match

Oxford U	15	Cambridge U	21

Women's University Match

Cambridge U	10	Oxford U	40

British Universities Final

Swansea U	35	St Mary's (Strawberry Hill)	15

British Universities Women's Final

Oxford U	10	Loughborough U	0

United Hospitals Cup Final

Imperial Medicals	21	Guy's, King's & St Thomas's	12

Scottish Amicable Trophy

Leicester	33	Barbarians	55

Cheltenham & Gloucester Cup Final

Gloucester	24	Bedford	9

Inter-Services Champions: The Army
Shell UK Ltd-Rosslyn Park Schools Sevens
Festival Winners: Wellington College
Open Winners: Stonyhurst College
Colts Winners: Millfield School
Junior Winners: Dwr-y-Felin School
Preparatory School Winners: Downsend
Girls' Winners: Welbeck College

Daily Mail Schools Champions: Colstons
Daily Mail U16 Schools Champions: Whitgift

Bread for Life Women's National Cup Final

Saracens I	44	O Leamingtonians	12

Women's National Champions: Saracens
Women's National 7s Winners: Saracens

HEINZ MEANZ TRIEZ

A GREAT SUPPORTER OF WORLD RUGBY

WALES

SWALEC Welsh Challenge Cup
Semi-finals

Cardiff	19	Llanelli	39
Cross Keys	3	Swansea	60

Final

Swansea	37	Llanelli	10

Welsh Challenge Trophy Final

Llanelli	41	Pontypridd	18

National Leagues
Premier Division

	P	W	D	L	T	B	Pts
GROUP 'A'							
Llanelli	20	15	1	4	104	18	64†
Pontypridd	20	12	0	8	80	10	46*
Neath	20	12	0	8	68	8	44†
Ebbw Vale	20	12	1	7	58	7	44*
GROUP 'B'							
Caerphilly	20	10	2	8	63	5	37†
Bridgend	20	9	2	9	61	5	34
Newport	20	5	0	15	63	8	23
Aberavon	20	2	0	18	51	4	10†

Relegated: Aberavon
* Denotes qualifier for European Cup
† Denotes qualifier for European Shield

First Division

	P	W	D	L	T	B	Pts
Dunvant	30	24	1	5	151	24	97
Bonymaen	30	22	2	6	120	32	91
Pontypool	30	23	0	7	101	11	80
Treorchy	30	16	2	12	113	14	64
Cross Keys	30	18	1	11	88	7	62
Merthyr	30	16	2	12	87	9	59
Llandovery	30	15	2	13	104	9	56
Tredegar	30	16	1	13	84	6	55
Rumney	30	12	1	17	92	14	51
Newbridge	30	14	0	16	71	6	48
Abertillery	30	12	2	16	69	10	48
UWIC (Card In)	30	12	1	17	74	5	42
Blackwood	30	10	1	19	87	9	40
Tondu	30	10	1	19	68	7	38
S Wales Police	30	9	1	20	70	1	29
Maesteg	30	2	0	28	45	2	8

Promoted: Dunvant
Relegated: South Wales Police, Maesteg.

2nd Division champions: Abercynon
Runners-up: Llanharan
3rd Div East champions: Glamorgan Wdrs
Runners-up: Bedwas
3rd Div West champions: Carmarthen Quins
Runners-up: Carmerthen Athletic

SCOTLAND

Tennents Super District Championship
*Edinburgh Reivers won series v Glasgow
Caledonians 2-1
(97-32 points aggregate)*

SRU Tennents Velvet Cup Final

Gala	8	Kelso	3

SRU Tennents Velvet Shield Final

Jed-Forest	35	Gordonians	23

SRU Tennents Velvet Bowl Final

Duns	34	Garnock	17

Scottish Sevens Winners:
Selkirk: Melrose
Kelso: Melrose
Melrose: Gala
Gala: Melrose
Hawick: Heriot's FP
Earlston: West of Scotland
Langholm: Melrose
Jed-Forest: Melrose
**Radio Borders/
   Borders Toyota Kings of Sevens:** Melrose

SRU Tennents Velvet Premiership
Division One

	P	W	D	L	F	A	B	Pts
Heriot's FP	18	14	0	4	620	322	13	69
Melrose	18	13	0	5	491	300	11	63
G Hawks	18	13	1	4	437	273	7	61
Currie	18	12	0	6	434	343	8	56
Hawick	18	9	0	9	338	460	5	41
Watsonians	18	7	2	9	396	428	6	38
Jed-Forest	18	7	2	9	356	449	3	35
B'muir	18	6	0	12	382	454	10	34
W of Scot'd	18	6	0	12	354	418	9	33
Stirling Cty	18	0	1	17	300	662	6	8

Relegated: Stirling County, West of Scotland

Division Two

	P	W	D	L	F	A	B	Pts
Gala	18	14	0	4	449	176	12	60
Kelso	18	14	1	2	436	235	8	66
Kirkcaldy	18	11	0	7	372	298	12	56
D'dee HSFP	18	8	1	9	446	431	8	38*
Biggar	18	8	1	9	249	341	4	38
A'deen GSFP	18	6	2	10	299	343	8	36
Selkirk	18	8	1	9	279	340	6	36*
M'burgh	18	7	0	11	379	475	6	34
Kilmarnock	18	6	0	12	329	475	7	31
E Acads	18	5	0	13	283	415	8	28

Promoted: Gala, Kelso
Relegated: Kilmarnock, E Academicals
* denotes four points deducted

Division Three champions: Peebles
Runners-up: Preston Lodge

IRELAND

Inter-Provincial Championship

	P	W	L	F	A	Bn	Pts
Munster	6	4	2	125	92	2	18
Ulster	6	3	3	137	119	3	15
Leinster	6	3	3	135	136	2	14
Connacht	6	2	4	95	145	3	11

Senior Provincial Cup Winners:
Connacht: Buccaneers
Leinster: Clontarf
Munster: Garryowen
Ulster: Instonians

AIB All-Ireland League
Division I

	P	W	D	L	F	A	Pts
Garryowen	11	8	0	3	237	140	16
Cork Const'n	11	8	0	3	265	170	16
Buccaneers	11	8	0	3	196	202	16
St Mary's Coll	11	7	0	4	215	177	14
Lansdowne	11	7	0	4	189	184	14
Shannon	11	6	0	5	224	164	12
Young Munster	11	4	1	6	134	135	9
Terenure Coll	11	4	1	6	175	182	9
Ballymena	11	4	0	7	190	224	8
Clontarf	11	4	0	7	198	246	8
Blackrock Coll	11	4	0	7	180	232	8
Galwegians	11	1	0	10	117	264	2

Champions: Cork Constitution
Relegated: Blackrock Coll, Galwegians

Division II

	P	W	D	L	F	A	Pts
Dungannon	15	13	0	2	479	259	26
De la S'e-P'ston	15	10	2	3	284	211	22
Wanderers	15	10	0	5	342	293	20
Old Belvedere	15	9	1	5	276	212	19
Malone	15	9	1	5	233	206	19
Bective Rangers	15	8	2	5	240	269	18
Portadown	15	8	1	6	253	268	17
Greystones	15	8	0	7	334	313	16
Old Crescent	15	7	1	7	305	236	15
Sunday's Well	15	7	0	8	270	246	14
City of Derry	15	7	0	8	284	293	14
Univ Coll Cork	15	5	4	6	248	303	14
Dolphin	15	5	1	9	218	256	11
Skerries	15	3	1	11	199	265	7
Old Wesley	15	2	2	11	181	315	6
Ballynahinch	15	1	0	14	171	372	2

Champions: Dungannon
Promoted: De la Salle-Palmerston
Relegated: Old Wesley, Ballynahinch

Division IIIA champions: Univ Coll Dublin
Division IIIB champions: Richmond
Division IV champions: Midleton

FRANCE

French Club Championship
Quarter-finals

Montferrand	36	Castres	31
Grenoble	28	Colomiers	26
Bègles-Bordeaux	8	Bourgoin	14
Toulouse	51	Stade Français	19

Semi-finals

Montferrand	26	Grenoble	17
Toulouse	26	Bourgoin	17

Final

Toulouse	15	Montferrand	11

French Cup
Semi-finals

Bègles-Bordeaux	20	Bourgoin	28
Stade Français	25	Pau	6

Final

Stade Français	27	Bourgoin	19

ITALY

Italian Championship
Final

Treviso	23	Padova	14

NEW ZEALAND

Championship First Division 1998
Semi-finals

Otago	61	Taranaki	12
Waikato	32	Canterbury	13

Final

Otago	49	Waikato	20

Ranfurly Shield Holders: Waikato

SOUTH AFRICA

Currie Cup 1998
Semi-finals

Blue Bulls	31	Natal	17
W Province	27	Griqualand West	11

Final

Blue Bulls	24	W Province	20

AUSTRALIA

National Championship 1998

New South Wales	41	Queensland	17

BARBARIANS

Opponents	Results
Combined Services	W 51-20
Leicester	W 38-24
East Midlands	W 51-19
Leicester	W 55-33

(Scottish Amicable Trophy)

Played 4 Won 4

SUPER-12 TOURNAMENT

Final Table

	P	W	D	L	F	A	Pts
Queensland Reds	11	8	1	2	233	170	38
Western Stormers	11	8	0	3	290	244	36
Otago Highlanders	11	8	0	3	280	203	35
Canterbury Crusaders	11	7	1	3	324	262	33
ACT Brumbies	11	5	0	6	278	195	28
Waikato Chiefs	11	5	0	6	248	301	26
Coastal Sharks	11	5	1	5	241	232	25
NSW Waratahs	11	4	1	6	246	248	24
Auckland Blues	11	4	1	6	202	201	23
Wellington Hurricanes	11	4	1	6	213	226	22
Golden Cats	11	4	0	7	312	341	22
Northern Bulls	11	1	0	10	203	447	7

Semi-finals

Q'land Reds　22　Cant Crusaders　28
(Brisbane)

W'n Stormers　18　Otago H'landers 33
(Cape Town)

Final

Otago H'landers 19　Cant Crusaders　24
(Dunedin)

PREVIEW OF THE SEASON 1999-2000

KEY PLAYERS 1999-2000

BY IAN ROBERTSON

ENGLAND

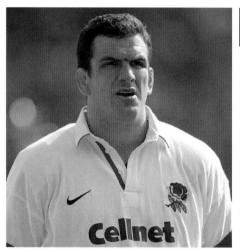

MARTIN JOHNSON

It is interesting to note that for all the supposed lack of glamour associated with playing in the second row many of the most celebrated names in rugby down through the years have been lock forwards. British players still tremble at the sound of the two words 'Colin Meads'. Willie John McBride captained the greatest-ever British Lions side in 1974, and English lock Bill Beaumont captained both England and the British Lions in 1980. Martin Johnson has now followed in Beaumont's footsteps and they have a lot in common. A successful captain of the British Lions in South Africa in 1997, Johnson leads by example on the field of play rather than by passionate Agincourt speeches off it. Last season he took over the captaincy when Lawrence Dallaglio was unavailable and it is not surprising he takes such responsibilities in his stride because he has enjoyed three years captaining Leicester. One of the best locks in world rugby, he is an outstanding line-out jumper, a fierce scrummager and a furious competitor. Above all, Martin Johnson is a team man, and England will be able to build a terrific pack around his formidable skills.

JONNY WILKINSON

It is hard to believe that just over two years ago Jonny Wilkinson was playing for England schoolboys and he enjoyed his first tour to Australia with England 18 Group in 1997. A natural fly half, he was unable to play in that position during his first two seasons of senior rugby with Newcastle because a player virtually twice his age called Rob Andrew not only had 70 England caps and two British Lions tours under his belt but also picked the Newcastle team and liked to play fly half. However, so multi-talented was young Wilkinson that he played most of the time in the centre and last season he shared the responsibilities of playing fly half with Rob Andrew. He won his first cap for England when he was still seven weeks short of his nineteenth birthday and has developed into a top-class international star with almost indecent haste. By the end of the Five Nations Championship last season he had scored 60 points for England and he looks sure to be a key player for a long time to come. He is a great defensive tackler, has good hands, kicks equally well with either foot, has a keen eye for a gap and is a world-class goal-kicker.

FRANCE

ABDELATIF BENAZZI

Having begun his international career with Morocco, he switched allegiance to France in time for the 1991 Rugby World Cup. He won his first three caps against Australia and his next two against New Zealand, so it really was a baptism of fire. He became an established member of the French team from 1991 right through to 1998, playing in 61 Tests in three different positions. Although he would probably agree that No. 8 is his best position, he has also played a lot of international rugby at flanker and lock. To some extent he has been a victim of his versatility and last season the French selectors dropped him. At the end of a disastrous Five Nations Championship in which France finished bottom of the table with three defeats against Wales, England and Scotland, Benazzi was recalled for the international against Romania in May. The French enjoyed a big victory. Benazzi is is a gifted ball player and he brings out the best in the players around him. He was arguably the best back-row forward in the 1995 World Cup and he is the sort of charismatic player France need now.

EMILE NTAMACK

A player of remarkable versatility, Emile Ntamack began his senior career with both Toulouse and France as a wing. He won his first full cap against Wales in 1994 and he helped France finish third in the 1995 Rugby World Cup when he scored a try in injury time in the crucial pool match to give his side victory over Scotland; he also scored a try in the quarter-final win against Ireland. The French failed to score a try in their semi-final defeat by South Africa, but switching from wing to full back in the third-place play-off game, he scored one of the two French tries in the win over England. Seemingly at the peak of his powers, he scored 13 tries for France in the two-year period starting with the 1995 World Cup, but having firmly established himself in the side as a potential match winner he has had a

wretched time with injuries and played only two full internationals in 1997 and 1998. Fit again last season, he was selected at full back, where his power and pace can be seen to devastating effect. Wherever the French play him, he remains, with Thomas Castaignède, one of their two best backs.

IRELAND

PADDY JOHNS

It was odd how the Irish pack promised so much in last season's Five Nations Championship and yet in the end they produced so little. They are able to boast two 1997 British Lions players in the front row – Paul Wallace and Keith Wood – and two top-class lock forwards in Paddy Johns and Jeremy Davidson, as well as a big, strong, mobile back-row. There is no doubt the potential is there, and considering the amount of experience among the tight five forwards, sooner or later they should be capable of laying the foundations for a series of good Irish wins at international level. Paddy Johns has played consistently well for Ireland in winning 50 caps for his country over a ten-year period. He won his first cap against Argentina way back in 1990, and since 1993 he has been the regular first-choice second-row forward. He is a good jumper and a strong scrummager; he excels in ruck and maul; and for a big man (6ft 6ins and 17½ stones) he is very effective around the pitch. He is a natural leader and has captained Ireland several times. This season he is back playing his rugby in Ireland and he should be a key member of the Irish team.

CONOR O'SHEA

Although he is one of the most experienced backs in the Irish team, it is only in the past two seasons that he has developed into one of the best full backs in the Northern Hemisphere. One of the reasons for his recent outstanding form has been the great resurgence at London Irish, where O'Shea has been in brilliant form throughout thet period. The open, fluent style that London Irish adopted last season helped to give O'Shea the attacking platform that he relished, and he was able to produce the same exciting performances at international level that he turned in week in and week out for the club. It should be said that he is also a very solid, reliable defensive player, but it is his attacking skills that have made him such a valuable player for both London Irish and Ireland. It is worth making the

point that he has benefited from having so many good players in the London Irish back division. With international half backs like Kevin Putt and Steve Bachop and Springbok Brendan Venter in the centre, the situation is made for a running full back.

ITALY

DIEGO DOMINGUEZ

Italy battled their way to prominence with a string of good performances against France in the late 1980s and early 1990s and then they followed up with some encouraging displays in the first three World Cups, as well as in a succession of one-off internationals against the four Home Unions. Well coached, they play very much as a team and this is probably their greatest strength, but they have also produced a handful of brilliant backs who have good enough skills to play at the highest level. The two who currently stand out are Diego Dominguez at fly half and Paolo Vaccari, who can play full back or wing. Diego Dominguez is one of the most talented fly halves of the 1990s. Safe of hand and a beautiful kicker of the ball, he is quick on the break, a master tactician and the ideal general to command his back division. He is also a phenomenally successful goal-kicker. Brought up in Argentina, he moved to Italy and won his first full cap in 1991 in a 15-9 win over France. He has played over 50 times for Italy and is their top points scorer in international rugby. Now 33, he is approaching the end of a distinguished career, but he is still the most important Italian back.

MASSIMO GIOVANELLI

Italy have had a good club league for the past 30 years but only have emerged as a potentially top rugby nation since the first RWC in 1987. A great deal of progress has been made in the last decade, and with their inclusion in the new Six Nations Championship the Italians have a wonderful opportunity to advance their cause. Their pack played some great rugby in the 1991 and 1995 World Cups; they looked like the French forwards, so good was their running, passing and support play. Their inspirational leader is Massimo Giovanelli, who plays his club rugby for Narbonne in France. He won his first cap as an explosive flanker against Zimbabwe in 1989 and he has been a regular first choice for Italy through the 1990s. He has now won over 50 caps and he has been captain for over half of those matches. A great character, he is a highly talented player who is equally forthright in attack and defence. He has played for the past two years for the World XV against the English Division One champions; this year in the Scottish Amicable Trophy match he looked very comfortable alongside Zinzan Brooke and François Pienaar in the BaaBaas back row.

SCOTLAND

JOHN LESLIE

In recent years the Scottish Rugby Union net, which used to stretch all round Scotland and across the border to England, has been cast wider to encompass most of the globe, including key areas such as New Zealand and South Africa. The find of last season was unquestionably the centre threequarter John Leslie, who began his rugby career in Otago in the south island of New Zealand, where he helped his province win the NPC title. He comes from an immaculate pedigree, as his father is Andy Leslie, who captained the All Blacks on ten occasions in the mid-1970s. John Leslie is a typical New Zealand centre in the mould of Bruce Robertson, Frank Bunce and Walter Little. He is a big, strong, powerful runner in attack as befits a player who is over 6ft tall and 15 stones in weight. With that build he is also a ferocious tackler, and he has that added priceless New Zealand commodity – he is furiously competitive. He rewrote the history books last season when he scored the fastest recorded Scottish try in international history. Scotland kicked off against Wales and nine seconds later Leslie touched down for the opening score.

SCOTT MURRAY

One of the main reasons for the dramatic resurgence in the fortunes of the Scotland rugby side last season was the emergence of the 23-year-old lock forward Scott Murray. It was reassuring for the pack to know that at every line out on a Scottish throw they had an outstanding jumper who was virtually guaranteed to win the ball. The Scottish front row has been solid and consistent and, especially with the arrival of Martin Leslie from New Zealand, the back row has produced the perfect blend of power, pace and footballing skill required at the highest level. Now the Scots have the ideal young lock to give strength in the engine room of the scrum and total command at the line out. Scott Murray is an excellent example of the new breed of modern professional lock who has all the virtues of the old-fashioned second-row forward combined with the mobility, athleticism and handling skills of a back-row player. He won his first cap in 1997 at the age of only 21 against Australia and he celebrated by scoring a try. He got his second try in the big win over Wales last season and he will be a most important forward for Scotland for many years to come.

WALES

SHANE HOWARTH

The Welsh have had the makings of a good back division for the past two or three years, but for all the great defensive ability of Scott Gibbs and Allan Bateman in the centre as well as their equally outstanding attacking skills and the speed and strength of their wings they had not been able to work out the best combination at fly half and full back. Last season, new coach Graham Henry was immediately able to see the problem and sort out the solution. Alongside Rob Howley at scrum half, Henry chose Neil Jenkins (hitherto a full back-cum-centre-cum-fly half) at fly half and introduced former New Zealand international Shane Howarth at full back. At a stroke the Welsh got a settled back division, and they can build on all the relative strengths of these players. Howarth won his first four caps for New Zealand in 1994 against South Africa and Australia; now domiciled in the UK, he won his first cap for Wales in 1998 against South Africa. He set a club record for Sale last year, scoring over 300 points in 30 games, but with Neil Jenkins around he does not kick for Wales. A great attacking full back, he has given Welsh rugby a new dimension and a new self-belief.

SCOTT QUINNELL

There is no doubt that for all his great rugby talent, Scott Quinnell is a bit of a mercurial maverick, and one of the most important tasks confronting the Welsh coach, Graham Henry, is to harness all that ability into an aggressive, disciplined performance. At his best, Scott is the ideal player around whom the coach can build his pack. He should be the apex of the whole Welsh forward thrust. He charges round the field like a wild rhino with the ball in his hands and he takes an awful lot of stopping. In defence, he represents a brick wall to the opposition. If he can combine these two sides of his character and produce a high work-rate for 80 minutes he would be a huge and priceless asset to the Welsh team. His tremendous strength and outstanding ball-handling skills are now ideally

complemented by the fleet-footed running and support play of new flanker Brett Sinkinson and the experienced Colin Charvis. Possessing a decent, if not exactly invincible, set of forwards, the Welsh pack should be good enough to give their talented back division a reasonable share of the ball, and the Welsh can look forward to the future with some confidence.

FIXTURES 1999-2000

Note: No venue given for a representative match indicates that the ground was yet to be announced at the time of going to press.

AUGUST 1999

Sat, 14th   Wales Domestic Weekend 1
Tue, 17th   Scotland 'A' v Argentina 'A' (Perth)
Sat, 21st   ENGLAND v USA
       (Twickenham, 7pm)
       SCOTLAND v ARGENTINA
       (Murrayfield)
       WALES v ROMANIA (Cardiff)
       Wales Domestic Weekend 2
Sat, 28th   ENGLAND v CANADA
       (Twickenham, 7pm)
       IRELAND v ARGENTINA (Dublin)
       SCOTLAND v ROMANIA
       (Hampden Park, Glasgow)
       WALES v FRANCE (Cardiff)
       Jewson Nat Lges 1/2 (1)
       Tetley's Bitter Cup (Prelim Rd)
       Scottish Premier Leagues (1)
       Wales Domestic Weekend 3

SEPTEMBER 1999

Sat, 4th   Jewson Nat Lges 1/2 (2)
       Scottish Premier Leagues (2)
       Scottish Nat Lges, all divs (1)
       Wales Domestic Weekend 4
Tue, 7th   ENGLAND XV v EFDR (Anfield)
       Allied Dunbar Premiership Two (1)
Sat, 11th   Allied Dunbar Premiership One (1)
       Allied Dunbar Permiership Two (2)
       Jewson Nat Lges 1/2 (3)
       National Leagues, England
       Scottish National Cup (1st Round)
       Scottish Premier Leagues (3)
       Scottish National Leagues 1-3 (2)
       Wales Domestic Weekend 5
Sat, 18th   ENGLAND XV v EFDR
       (Twickenham)
       Allied Dunbar Premiership Two (3)
       Jewson Nat Lges 1 (4)
       Tetley's Bitter Cup (1st Round)
       NPI Cup (1st Round)
       Tetley's Bitter Vase (1st Round)
       Scottish Premier Leagues (4)
       Scottish Nat Lges 1-3 (3); 4/5 (2)
       Wales Domestic Weekend 6
Sat, 25th   Allied Dunbar Premiership One (2)
       Allied Dunbar Premiership Two (4)
       Jewson Nat Lges 1/2 (5/4)
       National Leagues, England
       Scottish Premier Leagues (5)

Scottish Nat Lges 1-3 (4); 4/5 (3)
Wales Domestic Weekend 7

OCTOBER 1999

Fri, 1st   WALES v ARGENTINA
       (Cardiff, 3pm, RWC)
       FIJI v NAMIBIA
       (Béziers, 9pm, RWC)
       Scottish Premier Leagues (6)
       (Edinburgh & Borders)
Sat, 2nd   FRANCE v CANADA
       (Béziers, 2pm, RWC)
       SPAIN v URUGUAY
       (Galashiels, RWC)
       ENGLAND v ITALY
       (Twickenham, 5pm, RWC)
       IRELAND v USA
       (Dublin, 7pm, RWC)
       Allied Dunbar Premiership One (3)
       Allied Dunbar Premiership Two (5)
       Jewson Nat Lges 1/2 (6/5)
       National Leagues, England
       Scottish Premier Leagues (6)
       (Other Districts)
Sun, 3rd   WESTERN SAMOA v JAPAN
       (Wrexham, 1pm, RWC)
       NEW ZEALAND v TONGA
       (Bristol, 3pm, RWC)
       SCOTLAND v SOUTH AFRICA
       (Murrayfield, 5 pm, RWC)
       AUSTRALIA v ROMANIA
       (Belfast, 7pm, RWC)
Fri, 8th   SCOTLAND v URUGUAY
       (Murrayfield, 4pm, RWC)
       FRANCE v NAMIBIA
       (Bordeaux, 9pm, RWC)
Sat, 9th   FIJI v CANADA
       (Bordeaux, 1.30pm, RWC)
       WALES v JAPAN
       (Cardiff, 2.30pm, RWC)
       ENGLAND v NEW ZEALAND
       (Twickenham, 4.30pm, RWC)
       USA v ROMANIA
       (Dublin, 7pm, RWC)
       Allied Dunbar Premiership One (4)
       Allied Dunbar Premiership Two (6)
       Jewson Nat Lges 1/2 (7/6)
       National Leagues, England
       Scottish Premier Leagues (7)
       Scottish Nat Lges 1-3 (5); 4/5 (4)
Sun, 10th   ARGENTINA v WESTERN SAMOA
       (Llanelli, 1pm, RWC)
       IRELAND v AUSTRALIA
       (Dublin, 3pm, RWC)

SOUTH AFRICA v SPAIN
(Murrayfield, 5pm, RWC)
ITALY v TONGA
(Leicester, 7pm, RWC)
Thu, 14th   NEW ZEALAND v ITALY
(Huddersfield, 1pm, RWC)
WALES v WESTERN SAMOA
(Cardiff, 3pm, RWC)
AUSTRALIA v USA
(Limerick, 5pm, RWC)
CANADA v NAMIBIA
(Toulouse , 8.30pm, RWC)
Fri, 15th   ENGLAND v TONGA
(Twickenham, 1pm, RWC)
SOUTH AFRICA v URUGUAY
(Hampden Park, 5pm, RWC)
IRELAND v ROMANIA
(Dublin, 7pm, RWC)
Sat, 16th   FRANCE v FIJI
(Toulouse, 2pm, RWC)
SCOTLAND v SPAIN
(Murrayfield, 3pm, RWC)
ARGENTINA v JAPAN
(Cardiff, 7pm, RWC)
Allied Dunbar Premiership One (5)
Allied Dunbar Premiership Two (7)
Tetley's Bitter Cup (2nd Round)
NPI Cup (2nd Round)
Tetley's Bitter Vase (2nd Round)
Sun, 17th   Scottish National Cup (2nd Round)
Scottish Premier Leagues (8)
Wed, 20th   RWC Quarter-final Play-offs
(Twickenham, 1pm; Murrayfield,
3.30pm; Lens, 8.30pm)
Sat, 23rd   RWC First Quarter-final
(Cardiff, 3pm)
Allied Dunbar Premiership Two (8)
Jewson Nat Lges 1/2 (8/7)
National Leagues, England
Scottish Premier Leagues (9)
Scottish Nat Lges 1-3 (6); 4/5 (5)
Sun, 24th   RWC Remaining Quarter-finals
(Paris, 2pm; Dublin, 3.30pm;
Murrayfield, 6pm)
Sat, 30th   RWC First Semi-final
(Twickenham, 3pm)
Allied Dunbar Premiership One (6)
Jewson Nat Lges 1/2 (9/8)
Sun, 31st   RWC Second Semi-final
(Twickenham, 3pm)
Scottish Nat Lges 1-3 (7); 4/5 (6)*

NOVEMBER 1999

Thu, 4th   RWC Third-place Play-off
(Cardiff, 8pm)
†Sat, 6th   RWC Final (Cardiff, 3pm)
Allied Dunbar Premiership One (7)
Jewson Nat Lges 1/2 (10/9)
Sun, 7th   Scottish Nat Lges 1-3 (8); 4/5 (7)

Tue, 9th   Combined Services v Barbarians
(Gloucester)
Sat, 13th   Allied Dunbar Premiership One (8)
National Leagues, England
Scottish National Cup (3rd Round)
Wales Domestic Weekend 8
Sat, 20th   European Matches (1)
Allied Dunbar Premiership Two (9)
Jewson Nat Lges 1/2 (11/10)
National Leagues, England
Scottish Premier Leagues (10)
Scottish Nat Lges 1-3 (9); 4/5 (8)
Sat, 27th   European Matches (2)
Jewson Nat Lges 1/2 (12/11)
National Leagues, England
Allied Dunbar Premiership Two (10)
Scottish Premier Leagues (11)
Scottish Nat Lges 1-3 (10); 4/5 (9)
AIB League 2, 3 & 4 (1)
Mon, 29th   Scotland U21 XV v N Zealand U21

DECEMBER 1999

Wed, 1st   Scotland U21 XV v N Zealand U21
Sat, 4th   Allied Dunbar Premiership One (9)
Allied Dunbar Premiership Two (11)
Jewson Nat Lges 1/2 (13/12)
National Leagues, England
Scottish Premier Leagues (12)
Scottish Nat Lges 1-3 (11); 4/5 (10)
Wales Domestic Weekend 9
Dubai Sevens (Dubai)
AIB League 1 (1)
AIB League 2, 3 & 4 (2)
Tue, 7th   OXFORD v CAMBRIDGE
(Bowring Bowl, Twickenham)
Oxford U21 v Cambridge U21
(Bowring Plate, Stoop)
Sat, 11th   European Matches (3)
Allied Dunbar Premiership Two (12)
Jewson Nat Lges 1/2 (14/13)
NPI Cup (4th Round)
Tetley's Bitter Vase (4th Round)
Scottish Premier Leagues (13)
Scottish Nat Lges 1-3 (12); 4/5 (11)
AIB League 2, 3 & 4 (3)
Sat, 18th   European Matches (4)
Allied Dunbar Premiership Two (13)
Jewson Nat Lges 1/2 (15/14)
National Leagues, England
Scottish National Cup (4th Round)
AIB League 2, 3 & 4 (4)
Sun, 26th   Allied Dunbar Premiership One (10)
Tue, 28th   Wales Domestic Weekend 10
Leicester v Barbarians (prov)
AIB League 1 (2)
Malone v Blackrock (AIB 2)
Old Wesley v Skerries (AIB 3)
Wed, 29th   Allied Dunbar Premiership One (11)

* subject to Scotland's RWC progress.

† Matches on Saturday, 6 November in England may be rearranged and played by 2 January 2000 depending on RWC results.

JANUARY 2000

Sat, 1st	Wales Domestic Weekend 11
Sun, 2nd	Tetley's Bitter Cup (4th Round)
Sat, 8th	European Matches (5)
	Allied Dunbar Premiership Two (14)
	Jewson Nat Lges 1/2 (16/15)
	National Leagues, England
	Scottish National Cup (5th Round)
	AIB League 2, 3 & 4 (5)
Sat, 15th	European Matches (6)
	Allied Dunbar Premiership Two (15)
	Jewson Nat Lges 1/2 (17/16)
	NPI Cup (5th Round)
	Tetley's Bitter Vase (5th Round)
	National Leagues, England
	Scottish Premier Leagues (14)
	Scottish Nat Lges 1-3 (13); 4/5 (12)
	AIB League 2, 3 & 4 (6)
Sat, 22nd	Allied Dunbar Premiership One (12)
	Allied Dunbar Premiership Two (16)
	Jewson Nat Lges 1/2 (18/17)
	National Leagues, England (12-team divisions)
	Scottish Premier Leagues (15)
	Scottish Nat Lges 1-3 (14); 4/5 (13)
	Wales Domestic Weekend 12
	AIB League 1 (3)
	AIB League 2, 3 & 4 (7)
Tue, 25th	Allied Dunbar Premiership One (13)
Sat, 29th	Tetley's Bitter Cup (5th Round)
	NPI Cup (6th Round)
	Tetley's Bitter Vase (6th Round)
	Jewson Nat Lges 2 (18)
	National Leagues, England
	Scottish Premier Leagues (16)
	Scottish Nat Lges,1-3 (15); 4/5 (14)
	Wales Domestic Weekend 13
	AIB League 1 (4)
	AIB League 2 (8)
	Ards v Queens Univ Belfast (AIB 4)
	Dublin University v Bangor (AIB 4)

FEBRUARY 2000

Fri, 4th	England 'A' v Ireland 'A'
	England U21 v Ireland U21
	Eng Students v Ireland Students
	Italy 'A' v Scotland 'A'
	Italy U21 v Scotland U21
	Wales 'A' v France 'A'
	Wales U21 v France U21
Sat, 5th	ENGLAND v IRELAND (Twickenham, 2.30 pm)
	ITALY v SCOTLAND (Rome, 2 pm)
	WALES v FRANCE (Cardiff, 4 pm)
	Scottish Prem Lges (stand-by)

	Scottish Nat Lges 1-3 (s/by); 4/5 (15)
Wed, 9th	Lansdowne v St Mary's (AIB 1)
Sat, 12th	Allied Dunbar Premiership One (14)
	Allied Dunbar Premiership Two (17)
	Jewson Nat Lges 1/2 (19)
	National Leagues, England
	Scottish Nat Cup (Quarter-finals)
	Wales Domestic Weekend 14
	AIB League 1 (5)
	AIB League 2 (9), 3/4 (8)
Sun, 13th	Dolphin v UC Cork (AIB 2)
Fri, 18th	France 'A' v England 'A'
	France U21 v England U21
	France Students v Eng Students
	Ireland 'A' v Scotland 'A'
	Ireland U21 v Scotland U21
	Wales 'A' v Italy 'A'
	Wales U21 v Italy U21
Sat, 19th	FRANCE v ENGLAND (Paris)
	IRELAND v SCOTLAND (Dublin, 4 pm)
	WALES v ITALY (Cardiff, 2 pm)
Sat, 26th	Tetley's Bitter Cup (Quarter-finals)
	NPI Cup (Quarter-finals)
	Tetley's Bitter Vase (Quarter-finals)
	Allied Dunbar Premiership Two (18)
	Jewson Nat Lges 1/2 (20)
	National Leagues, England
	Scottish Premier Leagues (17)
	Scottish Nat Lges, all divs (16)
	Wales Domestic Weekend 15
	AIB League 1 (6)
	AIB League 2 (10)
	AIB League 3/4 (9)
Sun, 27th	Bohemians v Monkstown (AIB 3)

MARCH 2000

Fri, 3rd	England 'A' v Wales 'A'
	England U21 v Wales U21
	Eng Students v Wales Students
	Scotland 'A' v France 'A'
	Scotland U21 v France U21
	Italy 'A' v Ireland 'A'
	Ireland U21 v Italy U21
Sat, 4th	ENGLAND v WALES (Twickenham, 2.30 pm)
	SCOTLAND v FRANCE (Murrayfield, 2 pm)
	IRELAND v ITALY (Dublin, 4 pm)
	Scottish Prem & Nat Lges (s/by)
Wed, 8th	East Midlands v Barbarians (provisional, Northampton)
Sat, 11th	Allied Dunbar Premiership One (15)
	Allied Dunbar Premiership Two (19)
	Jewson Nat Lges 1/2 (21)
	National Leagues, England
	Scottish Premier Leagues (18)
	Scottish Nat Lges, all divs (17)

	Wales Domestic Weekend 16
	AIB League 1 (7)
	AIB League 2 (11)
	AIB League 3/4 (10)
Fri, 17th	France 'A' v Ireland 'A'
	France U21 v Ireland U21
	Italy 'A' v England 'A'
	Italy U21 v England U21
	Italy Students v Eng Students
	Wales 'A' v Scotland 'A'
	Wales U21 v Scotland U21
Sat, 18th	ITALY v ENGLAND (Rome, 2 pm)
	WALES v SCOTLAND (Cardiff, 4 pm)
	NPI Cup (Semi-finals)
	Tetley's Bitter Vase (Semi-finals)
	Jewson Nat Lges 1/2 (22)
	National Leagues, England (12-team divisions)
Wed, 22nd	BUSA Championships Finals (Twickenham)
Sun, 19th	FRANCE v IRELAND (Paris)
Sat, 25th	Allied Dunbar Premiership One (16)
	Allied Dunbar Premiership Two (20)
	Jewson Nat Lges 1/2 (23)
	National Leagues, England
	Scottish Nat Lges, all divs (18)
	Wales Domestic Weekend 17
	AIB League 1 (8)
	AIB League 2 (12)
Sat, 25th to Sun, 26th	Hong Kong Sevens
Wed, 29th	Army v RAF (Gloucester)
Fri, 31st	France 'A' v Italy 'A'
	France U21 v Italy U21
	Ireland 'A' v Wales 'A'
	Ireland U21 v Wales U21
	Scotland 'A' v England 'A'
	Scotland U21 v England U21
	Scotland Students v Eng Students

APRIL 2000

Sat, 1st	FRANCE v ITALY (Paris)
	IRELAND v WALES (Dublin)
Sun, 2nd	SCOTLAND v ENGLAND (Murrayfield)
	Scottish National Cup (Semi-finals)
	Scottish Prem & Nat Lges (s/by)
Wed, 5th	Wanderers v Blackrock Coll (AIB 2)
Sat, 8th	Tetley's Bitter Cup (Semi-finals)
	Allied Dunbar Premiership One (17)
	Allied Dunbar Premiership Two (21)
	Jewson Nat Lges 1/2 (24)
	National Leagues, England
	Melrose Sevens (Scotland)
	Wales Domestic Weekend 18
	AIB League 1 (9)

	AIB League 2 (13)
	AIB League 3/4 (11)
Wed, 12th	Scottish Prem Lges (stand-by)
Sat, 15th	European Cup & Shield (Quarter-finals)
	Allied Dunbar Premiership Two (22)
	NPI Cup Final (Twickenham)
	Tetley's Bitter Vase Final (Twickenham)
	Jewson Nat Lges 1/2 (25)
	National Leagues, England
	FIRA U19 Championships
	Lansdowne v Garryowen (AIB 1)
Tue, 18th	Allied Dunbar Premiership One (18)
Wed, 19th	RN v RAF
Sat, 22nd	Scottish Cup Finals (Murrayfield)
	Allied Dunbar Premiership One (19)
	Allied Dunbar Premiership Two (23)
	Jewson Nat Lges 1/2 (26)
	County Championship (area matches)
	Wales Domestic Weekend 19
	AIB League 1 (10)
	AIB League 2 (14)
	FIRA U19 Championships
	Home Unions U18 C'ships begin
Sat, 29th	Allied Dunbar Premiership One (20)
	Allied Dunbar Premiership Two (24)
	County Championship (area matches)
	Wales Domestic Weekend 20
	Rugby League Challenge Cup Final (Murrayfield)
	AIB League 1 (11)
	AIB League 2 (15)

MAY 2000

Sat, 6th	European Cup & Shield (Semi-finals)
	Allied Dunbar Premiership One (21)
	Allied Dunbar Premiership Two (25)
	County Championship (area matches)
	RN v Army (Twickenham)
Sat, 13th	Allied Dunbar Premiership Two (26)
	County Championship (Quarter-finals)
	Wales Domestic Weekend 21
Sat, 20th	Tetley's Bitter Cup Final (Twickenham)
	Allied Dunbar Premiership One (22)
	SWALEC Cup Final (Cardiff)
	County Championship (Semi-finals)
	Wales Domestic Weekend 22
Sat, 27th	European Cup & Shield Finals

JUNE 2000

Sat, 3rd	County Championship Final (Twickenham)

Mission Statement

The Wooden Spoon Society aims to enhance the quality
and prospect of life for children and young persons in the
United Kingdom who are presently disadvantaged either
physically, mentally or socially

Charity Registration No: 326691